Perspectives

The Interdisciplinary Series of
Physical Education and Sport Science

Volume 1

SCHOOL SPORT AND COMPETITION

Steve Bailey, Editor

Meyer & Meyer Sport

British Library Cataloguing in Publication Data
A catalogue record for this book is available from the British Library

School Sport and Competition/
Steve Bailey (ed.).
– Oxford : Meyer & Meyer Sport (UK) Ltd., 2000
(Perspectives – The Interdisciplinary Series of
Physical Education and Sport Science ; Vol.1)
ISBN 1-84126-019-3

© 2000 by Meyer & Meyer Sport (UK) Ltd
Oxford, Aachen, Olten (CH), Vienna,
Québec, Lansing/ Michigan, Adelaide, Auckland, Johannesburg, Budapest
Cover and Type exposure: Typeline, Dagmar Schmitz, Aachen
Editor: Steve Bailey
Managing Editor: Deena Scoretz
Layout and Typesetting: Deena Scoretz
Cover Design: axept, Berlin
Printed and bound in Germany by
Druckpunkt Offset GmbH, Bergheim
e-mail: verlag@meyer-meyer-sports.com
ISBN 1-84126-019-3

Perspectives - The Interdisciplinary Series of Physical Education and Sport Science
Volume 1, July 1999

SCHOOL SPORT AND COMPETITION

CONTENTS

Selected Sport Science Perspectives

SCHOOL SPORT AND COMPETITION

Contributing Authors

Steve Bailey (Editor)

Dr. Bailey holds a Bachelor of Education degree in Physical Education and English and a PhD in History (Physical Education). He has been a teacher of physical education for 19 years and was Director of Physical Education at Winchester College, England, for ten years. He has published and presented papers at conferences on: the modern Olympic Games, secondary physical education, sports history, technology in physical education. Books published include: 'Science in the Service of Physical Education and Sport'; 'Readings in Sports History'; and '100 Years of Physical Education 1899-1999'. He is currently contracted to write the History of the Paralympic Movement.

Anita L. Defrantz (Commentary)

Ms. Anita Defrantz was elected Vice President of the International Olympic Committee (IOC) in 1997. She has been an IOC member since 1986 and was an Executive Board member from 1992-1997. Additionally, she contributes to the Olympic Movement through involvement in numerous IOC Commissions and Chairs the IOC Women and Sport Working Group.

Correspondence regarding *Perspectives*:
ICSSPE/CIEPSS, Am Kleinen Wannsee 6, 14109 Berlin, Germany
Tel: +49 30 805 00360
Fax: +49 30 8056386
E-mail: icsspe@icsspe.org

A champion rower, she was team captain and bronze medal winner at the 1976 Summer Olympic Games in Montréal, and silver medallist in the World Rowing Championships in 1978. Ms. Defrantz is currently the President of the Amateur Athletic Foundation of Los Angeles.

Susan J. Gavron (Adapted Physical Activity)

Dr. Susan J. Gavron is an Associate Professor and Chairperson of the Sport Management, Recreation and Tourism Division in the School of Human Movement, Sport, and Leisure Studies at Bowling Green State University in Ohio, USA. She received her doctorate in adapted secondary special education at Indiana University in 1976.

Dr. Gavron has more than 20 years' experience working with individuals with disabilities from age 6 months through to adulthood – including work as a volunteer for Special Olympics, and 20 years experience in aquatics for senior citizens. She participated in the research advisory group for the USOC Committee on Sports for the Disabled, and has been involved in research of elite athletes with disabilities at national and international levels. Dr. Gavron also has extensive programming experience in physical education and leisure for individuals with disabilities.

Frieder Roskam (Facilities and Equipment)

Prof. Roskam is a certified teacher for sport and physical education (DSLV), architect (BDA) and landscape architect (BDLA). At the national level he has been a lecturer at the German Sports University in Cologne since 1957, and was the Head of the Sports Facilities Institute of the German Sports Federation (DSB) from 1953-1970. From 1971-1993 he was the Head of the Sports and Leisure Facilities Department of the Federal Institute for Sports Science, Germany, and has been the Chair of the Sports Facilities Committee of the German Standards Institution since 1972.

At the international level, Prof. Roskam has been involved in the International Association for Sports and Leisure Facilities (IAKS) since 1965, first as an Executive Board member and then as Honorary Secretary General. He has been Editor in Chief of "*sports facilities + swimming pools*" since 1967, and has been a member of the Sport and Environment Commission of the International Olympic Committee since 1997.

Paul De Knop (Sports Management)

Dr. De Knop received his PhD in Physical Education, and also graduated in Leisure Studies at the Free University of Brussels (VUB) Belgium. He earned Masters Degrees in Sports Sociology and Sports Management from the University of Leicester (UK). Currently he is a full-time professor at the VUB teaching on areas of sport, leisure and physical education from a socio-pedagogical perspective. He is the Head of the Youth Advisory Center for Sport, an interdisciplinary research and advisory Center, of the Department of Top-level Sport and Study. Dr. De Knop is the Secretary-General of the ICSSPE Sport and Leisure Committee, and a member of ISCPES, EASM, ICSS, NASS and BLOSO, the Flemish Sport Administrative body. His research interests include youth and sport, sport and ethnic minorities, sport and tourism, and sports management.

Paul Wylleman (Sports Management)

Dr. Wylleman received his PhD in Psychology (Sports Psychology). He is an Associate Professor at the Faculty of Physical Education and Physiotherapy at the Faculty of Psychology and Pedagogy of the Free University of Brussels (VUB), Belgium, teaching sports and exercise psychology, and psychology of leisure. He is also the Co-ordinator of the Department of Top-level Sport and Study where he works with, and counsels, elite student-athletes while they combine an academic and a high-level athletic career. His research interests are focussed upon inter-personal relationships in (competitive) sport, and the development of talented young student-athletes' sports careers.

Jo Van Hoecke (Sports Management)

Jo Van Hoecke graduated in Physical Education at the University of Ghent (RUG), Belgium, and in Sports Management at the Catholic University of Leuven (KUL), Belgium. He is an assistant at the Faculty of Physical Education and Physiotherapy at the Free University of Brussels (VUB), Belgium, involved in teaching and research concerning sports management , and sports marketing. His research interests are in quality management in sport organisations, sport sponsorship and other management and marketing related topics. Currently he is developing a model for evaluating Flemish gymnastics clubs named IKGym.

Kristine De Martelaer (Sports Management)

Kristine De Martelaer has been preparing her doctoral degree in Physical Education at the Faculty of Physical Education, Free University of Brussels (VUB) since 1997 and is a Licentiate in Leisure Agogics. She is currently working as a Doctor-Assistant at the same faculty. Since 1997 she has also been affiliated with the department of Kinesiology & Sport Pedagogics at the University of Ghent (RUG). Her research interests include sport pedagogy, physical education, sport and youth culture in general and swimming in particular, with a special interest in qualitative research.

Livin Bollaert (Sports Management)

Dr. Livin Bollaert has a PhD in Physical Education, and has also received a Masters in Leisure Studies, a Masters in Policy Planning and Futures Research, and a Masters in Marketing & Advertisement. He is the Director of the Research Unit "Leisure, Futures Research and Policy Planning" in the Faculty of Physical Education and Physiotherapy at the Free University of Brussels (VUB), Belgium, and also co-ordinates the sports management program. His research interests focus on consumer behaviour and policy planning in leisure, sports and tourism; the marketing approach of sports organisations, and the strategic policy planning of sports structures including the aspect of human resources management.

Herbert Haag (Pedagogy)

Prof. Dr. Herbert Haag is a Professor of Sport Pedagogy and Director of the Institute for Sport and Sport Sciences at the University of Kiel, Germany. He received his Master of Science in Physical Education at the University of Washington, USA, and completed his PhD in 1969. He was an Instructor and Assistant Professor at the Institute for Sport Science at the University of Tübingen, and full Professor for Sport Pedagogy at the University of Gießen and the University of Kiel. Prof. Haag was the first Director of the newly founded German Olympic Institute in Berlin from 1993-1996. His research emphasises curriculum and instruction in sport; evaluation of teaching and learning processes in sport; comparative sport pedagogy; scientific theory foundations of sport science and sport philosophy.

Prof. Haag is the Editor of the "International Journal of Physical Education" (A Review Publication) and the book series "Texts on the Theory of Sport Disciplines". He is also co-editor of "Foundations for the Study of Sport". Prof. Haag has various functions within the administration of sport, physical education, and sport science in Germany and internationally.

Roland Naul (Pedagogy)

Prof. Dr. Roland Naul is a Professor of Sport Science and Sport Pedagogy in the Department of Physical Education and Sport Sciences at the University of Essen, Germany, and he also heads the Willibald Gebardt Research Institute. He received his PhD from Münster University in 1978. His research interests include the history of physical education and cross-cultural studies in sport pedagogy. He has authored and co-authored more than 150 publications in sport pedagogy and sport history. Dr. Naul is a member of several national and international societies and editorial boards. He served on the International Committee of Sport Pedagogy, and the International Society of Comparative Physical Education and Sport as President and Vice-President (1992-1996).

Neil Armstrong (Physiology)

Professor Neil Armstrong is Head of the Department of Exercise and Sport Sciences and Director of the Children's Health and Exercise Research Centre at the University of Exeter, UK. The Centre was awarded a Queen's Anniversary Prize for Higher Education in 1998 in recognition of its research. His research interests lie in the fields of paediatric exercise science and physical education. He has published 8 books and over 300 other publications on these topics, and is the editor of the European Journal of Physical Education. Prof. Armstrong is a former Chair/President of both the British Association of Sport Sciences, and the Physical Education Association of the UK. He has chaired the PE/Sport Sciences Panel of the UK Research Assessment Exercise since its inception in 1992.

Maureen R. Weiss (Psychology)

Dr. Maureen R. Weiss is a Professor of Sport and Exercise Psychology and Program Director of Health and Physical Education in the Curry School of Education at the University of Virginia. Her research has focused on the psychological and social development of children and adolescents through participation in sport and physical activity, with particular interests in the areas of self-perceptions, motivation, observational learning, moral development, and the influence of significant others (parents, peers, coaches) on youth participation.

Dr. Weiss has published over 70 articles in refereed journals, 10 book chapters, and was a Guest Editor for a special issue of Pediatric Exercise Science on Social Psychological Factors Influencing Children's Physical Activity. She has co-edited 3 books: Competitive Sport for Children and Youths, Advances in Pediatric Sport Sciences, Vol. 2: Behavioral Issues (with Daniel Gould), and Worldwide trends in Youth Sport. Dr. Weiss has given over 50 invited lectures, 100 research presentations, and 100 workshops for coaches, administrators, and teachers. Weiss served as President for the Association for the Advancement of Applied Sport Psychology (AAASP) from 1996-1998. In 1998 she assumed Associate Editor duties for the Journal of Sport and Exercise Psychology.

C. Roger Rees (Sociology)

Prof. Dr. Rees teaches courses in the sociology and social psychology of sport, physical education, and the body at the Department of Health Studies, Physical Education and Human Performance Science, Adelphi University, USA. He has published five books and more than 50 articles and chapters in this field, including Lessons of the Locker Room: The Myth of School Sports (Prometheus, 1994), co-authored with Andrew Miracle. This book is a controversial review of the evidence for and against the claim that participation in high school sports "builds character". Dr. Rees has taught and lectured in Germany, England, Israel and South Africa where, in the summer of 1991, he led workshops on using sport to reduce racial and ethnic tensions. More recently he has been involved in a comparative study of the importance of sport and the body among German and American adolescents, and research on fair play in sport.

PERSPECTIVES, VOLUME 1:
SCHOOL SPORT AND COMPETITION

Editorial

Steve Bailey

The International Council for Sport Science and Physical Education has a long and distinguished career in providing publications for its members as well as for a wider audience. One successful vehicle for achieving its aims has been the *Sport Science Review,* originally called the *ICSSPE Review* when it was begun in the mid-1970s. Its purpose was initially to publish papers from conferences supported or organised by ICSSPE. The *ICSSPE Bulletin* had been in existence from a few years before, and it began as a vehicle to disseminate internal news of the International Council. It still reports on ICSSPE's initiatives and those of its members and partners, and now also includes research summaries, feature theme sections and 'spotlights' on sport science and physical education initiatives in specific regions of the world. As a means of offering more in-depth information, the *Sport Science Review* and the *ICSSPE Bulletin* were joined in the 1980s by *Sport Science Studies* and *Technical Studies*. The latter publication is very subject-specific, whereas the *Sport Science Studies* series includes reports and collections of papers that have been prepared by the various member organisations of ICSSPE.

The *Sport Science Review* undertook to publish twice a year, with each issue aiming to represent a selected area of sport science. A theme editor, who was responsible for inviting five people to provide a review of the area, co-ordinated the publication. Each discipline was represented every five

Correspondence to: Dr. Steve Bailey, Director of Physical Education, Winchester College, Morshead's, 33, St. Cross Road, SO23 9JA Winchester, United Kingdom years. This successful formula was popular with members and readers beyond the ICSSPE membership.

One limitation of a rotation of disciplines in the *Sport Science Review* was the tendency for readers only to read the issue relating to their own particular specialisation. This was not meeting the broader publication aims of ICSSPE; to promote, stimulate and co-ordinate scientific research in the field of physical education and sport throughout the world and to support the application of its results in various practical areas of sport. The 'umbrella function' of ICSSPE had been stressed in discussions, and this meant that there was a responsibility to help spread the knowledge more widely, and to encourage the blurring of boundaries, as far as practical, between the recognised disciplines of sport science.

The Editorial Board, meeting in Budapest in 1997, decided that the Council could better serve its readership by developing a truly multidisciplinary publication – one that encouraged sport scientists to read beyond their own narrower expertise and to thereby appreciate the work being done in other disciplines. The potential for overlap and co-operation is far greater in the present climate of communication technology and globalisation. How could the Editorial Board encourage this inter-disciplinary dialogue? There has long been a suspicion of true multidisciplinary research as almost impossible to carry out due to the problems encountered by incompatible methodologies. This may not be strictly true, but for the Editorial Board it was a question of trying to bring the very worthwhile material to a wider audience in order to promote the exchange of high-level research. Various possibilities were proposed, including a frequently published news-stand-type magazine; one which would be bought by the serious sportsman as well as sport scientists. But this did not seem to set itself apart from the *Bulletin* and did not suit the purposes of the Editorial Board.

The structure of the new publication, *Perspectives: The Multidisciplinary Journal of Physical Education and Sport Science,* needed to step beyond a basic reportage of research papers. It was agreed to adopt a theme for each issue, and to invite authors from different disciplines from within sport science to present significant peer-reviewed papers on the theme. There was a need for high level academic content, but also a need for the avoidance of technical jargon so as to be clear to readers unfamiliar with that discipline. The authors were asked to show the relevance of their area of sport science to the selected theme, while identifying and outlining relevant research in their discipline. Where possible authors have been asked to project future directions and possible developments of research in their area relating to the theme selected for that issue. A comprehensive bibliography is also important for further reference. It was thought beneficial to try to present two-tier bibliographies if possible; so as to encourage non-specialists to pursue further reading at an appropriate level for their knowledge. The content itself should be presented in the language of the non-specialist, making the material accessible to all.

A commentary paper has also been invited. This is not necessarily to be written by a sport scientist, but the author should help round the circle of knowledge and opinion. There is an effort to guide theory into practice, to suggest future areas of interaction and partnership. Possible paradigms for exploration may emerge from these presentations.

How have we constructed this first collection? Anita DeFrantz states her personal view of school sport and competition in the Commentary for this issue of *Perspectives*. Through her example and experience she is well qualified to explore the pitfalls and benefits of the role of competition in a school context. Sue Gavron has presented an admirable review of the theme in relation to Adapted Physical Activity. The world of sports equipment and facilities is represented by Frieder Roskam who, for many years, has been involved in the work of the International Council of Sport Science and Physical Education through the IAKS organization. Livin Bollaert brings the relatively new discipline of Sport Management to our compilation, making important comment about the interdisciplinary possibilities in these sorts of investigations. Roland Naul and Herbert Haag have written from the perspective of Sport Pedagogy, taking different starting points that in the end complement each other's work. Neil Armstrong's essay is a strong endorsement of the importance of the sort of physiological work that is being done at the moment to investigate child health and welfare as a result of changing attitudes and provision for physical activity in schools. The psychological angle is approached by Maureen Weiss, who manages to retain an interdisciplinary outlook while discussing adolescent and youth competition. Finally, Roger Rees combines historical, anthropological and sociological approaches to reveal the myths and rituals of school sports in America that are often taken for granted.

Altogether this first issue of *Perspectives: The Multidisciplinary Series of Physical Education and Sport Science* provides a new way of looking at the subject of School Sport and Competition. Rather than specialists perpetuating the inaccessibility of their subject matter by continual use of technical jargon and exclusive reference, we have pieced together a collection of related essays that encourage access to each defined discipline of Sport Science through the common interest in one theme.

Perspectives, 1999, Vol. 1: 17-20
School Sport and Competition

SCHOOL SPORT AND COMPETITION

Commentary

Anita L. DeFrantz

I believe that sport belongs to us all. It is something that we do as human beings. Sport involves a powerful form of thoughts as the mind directs the body through the dimensions of time and space. And, sport is a powerful force for community throughout the world.

My opportunity to take part in organized sports came with my entry to Connecticut College. Sport enriched my college life, and later my life at law school. I realized that this opportunity to take part in sport had been denied to me and I knew how I should work to make a change for others.

When I was a little girl we had physical education classes in school. I had the opportunity to run and jump and play kickball. But, by the time I was ready for organized sport, only boys had the opportunity to play. This was the case both in school and outside of school in sports clubs. I am very happy that now, in the United States, girls and boys have access to play sport. In fact girls now expect to take part in sport not only as children but continuing through adulthood.

Sadly, though, over the recent years, fewer and fewer opportunities for sport exist within the curricula of primary and secondary schools. It seems that sport is one of the first activities cut when the budgets of schools are tight. I

Correspondence to: Anita L. DeFrantz, Vice-President, International Olympic Committee, President, Amateur Athletic Foundation of Los Angeles, 2141 West Adams Boulevard, Los Angeles, California 90018, USA believe that this is a very bad choice. We have much to learn from sport. The thought that powers the body through the dimensions of time and space has yet to be thoroughly explored. We often celebrate an athlete whose performance has been exquisite. In the United States, we speak of "being in the zone". This refers to the zone of excellence, when a sporting performance nears or meets perfection. These moments of excellence are not reserved only for elite athletes. Even a child who is learning a skill for the first time can experience that moment of sublime excellence. Sports can help us understand how to get there, and perhaps someday teach us how to stay in a state of excellence.

My experience is that the field of play is an important classroom. Whether you are learning history or how to row, you are acquiring new skills and knowledge. You will then be tested and asked to do your best. Student athletes who must manage work in academics and sports display a high degree of dedication, discipline and self-esteem. They also learn teamwork and the appreciation of rewards for hard work. There is a recognition that success can be incremental improvement. Victories may come and go, but success is an experience to be built upon.

Student athletes acquire and learn to use the tools necessary to be productive members of society. Sport also teaches other important social lessons. At the Amateur Athletic Foundation of Los Angeles we have learned that sport is a very important factor for helping children feel a part of society. Los Angeles is a city where there is no majority group. People come to live in Los Angeles from all parts of the world. Often their parents may not have command of the English language and they rely on their children to communicate. But, the language of sport is universal. The desire to have one's children enjoy and experience success also is universal.

It is important however, to make sure that the emphasis in school sport is placed on the teaching and learning aspects of skills and not on the results of competition. As President of the Amateur Athletic Foundation of Los Angeles I place a great emphasis in ensuring that the coaches we train understand the philosophy, of "Athletes First, Winning Second".

Competition is a means to gauge the progress the athletes have made in acquiring and practising specific sport skills. Wins and losses should not be the most important measurement of a child's development in a sport.

While the opportunities for sports participation must be made available to every child, it is the right of every individual to choose to participate. This decision is often influenced by parents, coaches, school administrators and certainly by the media. The sports media glorifies those who succeed but just as quickly castigates those who fall from favour. The economics of today's sports, and the millions of dollars available to super star athletes, are a siren call to young people. For those who heed the call, success on the playing field is equated to great financial rewards. Unfortunately only a few athletes ever achieve the super star status. Educators, parents and coaches have the responsibility to assist student athletes in finding a balance between their educational goals and the pursuit of sport only as means to great financial wealth. Student athletes must not become the pawns in an institution's quest for sports championships. Ultimately it is the responsibility of a school to ensure that the education of the mind and body is taking place for the benefit of the student.

Successful student athletes bring glory to their institution. Every student athlete who has made the choice to participate in sport and represent the school should be given the best available training and advice so that they may achieve their potential. This is not different from providing the best professors and advisors for those studying other subjects.

The Olympic Games is a celebration of human excellence. Each quadrennial, athletes from every corner of the world gather to test themselves and become part of history. Each athlete who competes in the Games has taken his or her own road to get there. What they each have in common is the goal to become an Olympic champion. I, too, had the goal as I began my rowing career at Connecticut College. At the 1976 Olympic Games I earned a bronze medal. I continued to strive for the gold but the opportunity was snatched from me with the United States boycott of the 1980 Olympic Games.

Through the experience and knowledge I gained through education and participation in sports I had the expertise and courage to fight against the boycott. I believed then, and I believe to this day, that the decision to participate belonged to the athletes. I lost that fight, but the road I embarked upon through that struggle has led me to my present position as Vice President of the International Olympic Committee. Now my work for sport is both local and world-wide.

The benefits of participating in school sport are many. It is my wish that every student athlete has the opportunity to gain a valuable academic education while pursuing his or her goal in sport. There are many positive advantages gained from this pursuit. But, those advantages do not simply materialize. As in everything else in life they must be earned.

Anita L. DeFrantz
Vice President, International Olympic Committee
President, Amateur Athletic Foundation of Los Angeles.

Perspectives, 1999, Vol. 1: 21-31
School Sport and Competition

SCHOOL SPORT AND COMPETITION:
ADAPTED PHYSICAL ACTIVITY

Susan J. Gavron

Introduction

As a universal phenomenon, sport is a political, economic, and social force throughout the world (McPherson, Curtis & Loy, 1989). Major competitive sporting events such as the Olympics, The World Cup, International Tennis events, and other sport specific world championships are but just a few of the many elite events one may call to mind. In order for these events to take place there is, most often, a ladder or route an athlete must follow in terms of getting to this elite level of competition. Most often elite athletes get their start as young children with after school or local recreation experiences. But this is not necessarily true for all athletes. For those children and youth with disabilities the sporting experience may be non-existent, unknown, or just out of reach (DePauw, 1990; DePauw & Gavron, 1995).

Just what constitutes competitive sport in the public (state) school for children with disabilities? How has it developed? What are the benefits for children and youth with disabilities and are they the same as for able-bodied children? What are the barriers to participation in competitive sport for children and youth with disabilities? What is the role of adapted physical activity? A brief look at some of these parameters with reference to the

Correspondence to: Dr. Susan J. Gavron, Assoc. Prof. & Chair, Sport Management, Recreation & Tourism Division in the School of Human Movement ,Sport & Leisure Studies, Bowling Green State University, Gertrude M. Eppler Complex, BGSU, Bowling Green, OH 43403 USA.

United States will enable one to gain a perspective on what yet needs to be accomplished.

Historical Perspective of Competitive School Sport

In the United States, "a free and appropriate" public (state) school education is promised to all children (Federal Register, 1989). However, this promise of a public school education does not necessarily take into account nor accommodate those children and youth with disabilities as relates to competitive sport experiences. Early competitive sport experiences for school aged youth was very popular in the beginning of the 20th century, especially for white, male Christians (Wiggins, 1996). The period from the late 1880s through to the early 1920's found a variety of institutions involved in providing youth with opportunities for competitive sport. These institutions included, but were not limited to, the YMCAs, public school athletic leagues, and recreation programs. The competition was often intense (Wiggins, 1996). At the same time, in 1924, the First World Games for athletes with hearing impairments took place in Paris, France (DePauw & Gavron, 1995). These games are the oldest, continuous competitive games for people with disabilities.

While competitive sport opportunities for male children and youth was a staple of the early public school years, the 1930's saw professional leaders from Health, Physical Education, and Recreation at the state and national level condemn the existence of highly competitive sport at the elementary and junior high levels (Wiggins, 1996). In looking at marginalized groups such as girls and women, and those with disabilities, there is a different history. Competitive sport for girls and women in the public schools was non-existent in the early part of the century. Later during the 1940's and until the early 1960's the competitive sport experience took on the "playday" philosophy that competition was allowable, but only in highly controlled circumstances of short duration. For those with disabilities competitive public school sport opportunities, similar to those of their peers, was non-existent. However, it is important to acknowledge that there was limited school-aged sport competition between state schools for individuals with visual and hearing impairments (Winnick, 1990). These students were totally separated from the mainstream and usually were boarding at these schools, a situation not common to their peers. In reality it took another great war (World War II) for the emergence of competitive sport to be recognized as a legitimate enterprise for people with disabilities (DePauw & Gavron, 1995).

In the public school sector the 1950's saw an upheaval in terms of accommodation of people with differing abilities due to significant court cases and social change (Sherrill, 1998). In particular, in 1968 the first Special Olympics held at Soldier's Field in Chicago, Illinois, was a significant event for people with disabilities (DePauw & Gavron, 1995). For the first time children, youth, and adults with mental retardation were provided a national forum in the United States to demonstrate their abilities as athletes. In American society the ability to move and move well is a valued aspect.

Currently a trend towards inclusion in competitive school sport is in progress in the United States (DePauw & Gavron, 1995; Sherrill, 1998). Special Olympics promotes its "unified teams", and adolescents with physical disabilities have the opportunity to compete as wheelchair racers in local and national races such as the Boston Marathon, New York Marathon and state-wide open competitions such as the New York State Summer Games. However, more research with school aged youth is needed to ascertain the effect of these integrated experiences on both athletes with disabilities and able-bodied athletes.

Barriers to Participation

The road to inclusion into the competitive sport experience during the school aged years is fraught with barriers. Research has identified some of these barriers as:
- paucity of organized sport programs
- lack of early formal and informal sport experiences
- limited role models
- not enough trained coaches and training programs
- economics
- stigmatization
- type of government
- negative social attitudes towards people who are differently abled

- lack of information for power groups such as parents, physicians, and children's hospitals (Murphy & Charboneau, 1987; Karas & DePauw, 1990; DePauw & Gavron, 1995; Sherrill, 1998).

The fact that only 15 percent of people are born with congenital disability (Sherrill, 1998) may also have an impact on the number of children and youth available to participate in competitive sport. For most people with disabilities their competitive sport experience comes after their disability occurs. In the United States most occurrences of disability are during the teen years through to age 25-30 due to trauma (Gavron, 1989b).

The Role of Adapted Physical Activity

Adapted physical activity in the United States mainly takes place in the public schools at the elementary level, grades one to six, ages 5-11. During the junior high years, grades seven to nine (ages 12-15), there is less opportunity for specialists in adapted physical activity to be employed, and at the high school level, grades ten to twelve (approximately ages 16-18), there is little or no employment of adapted physical activity specialists. With this picture in mind, the encouragement and resources for a child or youth with a disability appears to diminish as they continue through their public school years. This pattern would then result in a definitive lack of participation of children and youth in competitive sport, which is the current case. Previous research by Gavron (1989b) and DePauw & Gavron, (1991) found that physical educators in the public schools were not the main impetus for young adult elite athletes with disabilities engaging in sporting experience. Rather, their family, friends, and perhaps another person with a disability were found to be a key to their involvement. A lack of trained coaches for disability sport was also noted at this stage.

Is the lack of influence by physical educators indicative of a lack of interest? Most likely it is a lack of information and training more than anything else. Those specially trained in adapted physical activity become a very significant part of the information and education flow about opportunities available in competitive sport for children and youth with disabilities. They also need to empower the parents of the children and youth to become involved, and to educate those physicians, physical therapists, occupational therapists, and others who support these children, to encourage them to become more active (Jansma and French, 1996).

The answer to involvement in competitive school sport for children and youth with disabilities is to view the entire situation and utilize some of the proven "best practices" for inclusion:

- find a learning channel (e.g. auditory, visual, or combination) that best fits the child
- change the class format to be more inclusive by utilizing small groups and less waiting time
- utilize peer tutors
- modify complexity of tasks
- utilize verbal and/or physical prompts
- manually manipulate body parts through the range of motion
- utilize equipment which is softer and lightweight, e.g. yarn balls, balloons, lightweight plastic balls
- change the height of nets and baskets to ensure early success
- make games and activities age-related and socially appropriate
- adapt rules to ensure no one is eliminated, but do not alter the essence of the activity
- shorten distances
- slow down the pace of the activity
- reduce distractions (Block, 1994; Rich, 1990; Gavron, 1989a; Sherrill, 1998).

When all other ideas fail to come to fruition it is always appropriate to ask the child with a disability or student co-learners for ideas. Many times they can offer excellent suggestions.

What next?

The sport experience for elite, young adult, and adult athletes with disabilities has been undergoing increased study since the mid-1980s. It was then that a research agenda was proposed for increasing the understanding and knowledge of disability sport (DePauw, 1986). The explosion of research about elite athletes with disabilities since that time is encouraging (Depauw, 1988; DePauw & Gavron, 1995). However it is noted that research on the benefits, performance, and biopsychosocial aspects of competitive school sport is clearly lacking for school-aged children and youth. There are several possibilities for this:

- lack of children and youth with disabilities involved in competitive sport in the public schools
- lack of interest by researchers
- difficulty in obtaining entrance into the public schools for research
- parental wariness of the research process
- lack of funding for research
- lack of a definitive lifelong, inclusive sport model and philosophy.

Encouraging practitioners to report their successes, along with the continued research of doctoral students and established scholarly professionals, may help alleviate some of these problems.

Another view of the increased availability of the sport experience for children and youth with disabilities will rest upon the role of adapted physical activity. A global understanding of adapted physical activity as a lifelong endeavor may enhance the opportunities for children with disabilities in all countries, regardless of culture. A model which is not medically oriented but looks at the total environment may also be a key. Steadward (1995) proposed that athletes are represented by the level and purpose of their athletic involvement - amateur, elite, or recreational. If we also look at the role of geography, economics, and culture we may find that all of these may interact according to the needs of each country and its youth.

The common denominator is sport, and all children with disabilities should have the opportunity for involvement whether it is legislated or not. People need to be sensitized towards accepting children and youth with disabilities as having the same wants and needs as their able-bodied peers. People need to understand that the "sporting experience" is not just for those elite athletes of the Olympics. We must train more of our young professionals to be able to work with those with disabilities as do those who specialize in adapted physical activity. We need to continue to have our national, regional, and global conferences in adapted physical activity and sport. We need to make sure that these conferences are inviting to the newly initiated as well as those with experience. We need to make sure that the ongoing activism for equal opportunity for all is continued. Maybe then the concept of adapted physical activity as a lifelong endeavor will be more meaningful. This will be a truly inclusive phrase, and the need for legislation to make things happen will be a thing of the past.

References

Block, M. E. (1994). *A teacher's guide to including students with disabilities in regular physical education*. Baltimore, MD: Paul H. Brooks.

DePauw, K. P. (1986). Research on sport for athletes with disabilities. *Adapted Physical Activity Quarterly*, **3**, 282-299.

DePauw, K. P. (1988). Sport for individuals with disabilities: research opportunities. *Adapted Physical Activity Quarterly*, **5**, 80-89.

DePauw, K. P. (1990). Sport, society and individuals with disabilities. In G. Reid (Ed.), *Problems in movement control* (pp.319-337). NY: Elsevier.

DePauw, K. P. & Gavron, S. J. (1991). Coaches of athletes with disabilities. *Physical Educator*, **48**, 33-40.

DePauw, K. P. & Gavron, S. J. (1995). *Disability and sport*. Champaign, IL: Human Kinetics.

Federal Register, June 22, 1989, PL99-457, *The Education of the Handicapped Act*. United States Congress.

Gavron, S. J. (1989A). Surviving the least restrictive environment. *Strategies*, **2** (3),5-6,28.

Gavron, S. J. (1989B). Early play and recreational experiences of elite athletes with disabilities of the VII Pan Am Games. Paper presented at the VII International Symposium in Adapted Physical Activity, Berlin, June, 1989.

Jansma, P. & French, R. (1994*). Special physical education: physical activity, sports, and recreation.* Englewood Cliffs, NJ: Prentice-Hall.

Karwas, M. R. & DePauw, K.P. (1990). Parallels between the women's and disabled sport movements. *Abstracts of Research Papers, 1990 AAHPERD Convention*. Reston, VA: American Alliance for Health, Physical Education, Recreation and Dance.

McPherson, B. D.; Curtis, J. E., & Loy, J.W. (1989). *The social significance of sport, an introduction to the sociology of sport.* Champaign, IL: Human Kinetics.

Murphy-Howe, R. & Charboneau, B. G. (1987*). Therapeutic recreation intervention, an ecological perspective.* Englewood Cliffs, NJ: Prentice-Hall.

Rich, S. (1990). Factors influencing the learning process. In J. Winnick (ed.). *Adapted physical education and sport* (pp.121-130). Champaign, IL: Human Kinetics.

Sherrill, C. (1998). *Adapted physical activity, recreation and sport, cross-disciplinary and lifespan.* (4th ed.).Boston, MA: WCB, McGraw-Hill.

Steadward, R. D. (1996). Integration and sport in the Paralympic movement. *Sport Science Review*, **5** (1),26-41.

Wiggins, D. K. (1996). A history of highly competitive sport for American children. In F.L. Smoll & R.E. Smith (Eds.), *Children and youth in sport, a biopsychosocial perspective* (pp. 15-30). Dubuque, IA: Brown & Benchmark.

Winnick, J. P. (ED) (1990). *Adapted physical education and sport.* Champaign, IL: Human Kinetics.

Non-Specialist References

Applied

Adams, R. C. & McCubbin, J.A. (1991). *Games, sports and exercises for the physically disabled* (4th ed.). Philadelphia, PA: Lea & Febiger.

Carter, M. J.; Browne, B.; LeConey, S. P. & Nagle, C. J. (1991). *Designing therapeutic recreation programs in the community.* Reston, VA: American Alliance for Health, Physical Education, Recreation, and Dance.

Grosse, S.; Cooper, C.; Gavron, S; Huber, J. & Stein, J (EDS.). *Sport instruction for individuals with disabilities*. Reston, VA: American Alliance for Health, Physical Education, Recreation and Sport.

Goodman, S. (1993) *Coaching athletes with disabilities: general principles.* Canberra, NSW: Australian Sports Commission.

Grosse, S. J. & Thompson, D. (Eds.) (1993). *Leisure opportunities for individuals with disabilities, legal issues.* Reston, VA: American Alliance for Health, Physical Education, Recreation, and Dance.

Grosse, S. J. & Thompson, D. (Eds.). (1993). *Play and recreation for individuals with disabilities, practical pointers.* Reston, VA: American Alliance for Health, Physical Education, Recreation, and Dance.

Paciorek, M. J. & Jones, J. A. (1989). *Sports and recreation for the disabled; a resource manual.* Indianapolis, IN: Benchmark Press.

Journals:

Adapted Physical Activity Quarterly, a research based publication which includes disability sport content.

Palaestra, The forum of sport, physical education and recreation for the disabled.

Sports and Spokes, The magazine for wheelchair sports and recreation.

Research:

Kozub, F. M. & Poretta, D. L. (1998). Interscholastic coaches' attitudes toward integration of adolescents with disabilities. *Adapted Physical Activity Quarterly*, **15** (4),328-345.

Klein, R. (1998). Design and use of adapted training bicycles for children with special needs. Paper presented at the North American Federation of Adapted Physical Activity Symposium in Minneapolis, MN, October 3, 1998.

Megginson, N. L. & Lavay, B. (1998). Perceived competency levels of adapted physical educators toward disability sport. Paper presented at the North American Federation of Adapted Physical Activity Symposium, Minneapolis, MN, October 3, 1998.

Reid, G. & Prupas, A. (1998). A documentary analysis of research priorities in disability sport. *Adapted Physical Activity Quarterly*, **15**(2), 168-179.

Stopka, C. (1998). Effects of an integrated program of physical fitness and sport activities on students with mental retardation. Paper presented at the North American Federation of Adapted Physical Activity, Minneapolis, MN. October 3, 1998.

SCHOOL SPORT AND COMPETITION: SPORTS FACILITIES

Hardware for Sports Education and Sport for All

Frieder Roskam

Introduction

In traditional conceptions of Shangri-La, not only do milk and honey flow, but the climate is also exceptionally mild. To pursue sport here – be it at school, in sports clubs or in other organized groups – one would merely need levelled surfaces, for there would be no need to worry about protection from the wind, rain, snow and sun. However, in the real world it is these natural elements which make structural protection necessary if such facilities are expected to cater for a large number of sports, permit continuous seasonal or all-year use, and accommodate the necessary additional functional rooms for athletes, equipment, technical installations and, possibly, spectators.

This statement is not mitigated by the fact that a number of sports can be practised in the open countryside. For the vast majority of sports disciplines, structures ranging from the sports surface through to the complete weatherproof enclosure of the field of action are essential. This realization is not new, but there is a growing trend towards considering sports facilities for Sport for All as not being absolutely imperative. One of the reasons for this trend is firstly the desire to practise sport in the natural environment, which, secondly, has been accompanied above all by the appreciation that building and maintaining sports facilities costs a lot of money. And money is

Correspondence to: Prof. Frieder Roskam, Secretary General, IAKS, Carl-Diem-Weg 3, 50933 Köln, Germany universally in short supply, if one ignores the spectacular large-scale facilities for which, in certain circumstances, the funding is provided solely for reasons of prestige.

One thing is certain: in the majority of countries sports facilities are still a rarity and particularly, of course, in the less developed countries and in Eastern Europe. In other countries sports facilities are available for schools and for clubs, although these are only accessible to certain groups of users. If we are convinced that sport is an important aspect of education – we need only think of physical exercise and the teaching of social behaviour – contact with sport in kindergartens and in schools should be part of all schoolchildren's curriculum. Areas and rooms therefore have to be created in which this education can take place.

In kindergartens these tend to be relatively small areas and rooms, some of which permit multifunctional use going beyond games for physical exercise. In schools, depending on the school type, these are larger units. Particularly at secondary schools these are large enough to meet the movement needs of most, if not all, adult age groups. For the elderly and certain groups established for the restoration of health, e.g. cardiac groups, cancer groups, the spatial requirements are again similar to those in primary schools and kindergartens.

From this point of view the hardware for physical education and sports education in the widest sense is indeed suitable for Sport for All. This hardware must be designed and equipped for multifunctional use and operation.

Requirements of facilities for school sport

Taking into account different age groups, the requirements are based on the specifications of the curricula of the school authorities and above all on the specified sports, and the associated dimensions, equipment and group size. The facilities should not only permit compulsory physical education. With the aim of encouraging young people to pursue sport for the rest of their lives, class instruction should also be supplemented by activities for interest and performance groups.

The need for a diversity of activities - a number of different types of sport - can only be satisfied by a multifunctional sports facility. This would be a facility which, with simple means and rapid conversion, is suitable for the staging of many different sports: a facility which may also be available for non-sports use, i.e. for the cultural and social events of the school and the school community.

Figure 1: Indoor sports hall (Stephan Y. Dietrich, Berlin)

In many climatic regions *covered sports facilities* are essential to enable pedagogical compliance with the desired curriculum. These are in most cases sports halls (Figure 1). Here preference should go to partitionable halls rather than single-space halls. Additional sports rooms such as gymnastics, fitness and stamina training rooms should be incorporated if possible from the outset in the allocation of rooms.

Figure 2: Outdoor playing field (polytan Sportstättenbau GmbH, Niederlassung Nord, Halle/Westf.)

With regard to *outdoor facilities*, small playing fields, suitable for games and athletic exercises (Figure 2), have priority over large pitches and complex facilities with 400m oval tracks. The latter are desirable at central locations for the preparation of athletes and the holding of school sports days. Apart from the small playing fields, grassed areas demarcated with earthworks or vegetation should be created for gymnastics and a variety of informal games (Figure 3).

Figure 3:   Grassed area for games and gymnastics (Landessportbund Hessen, Frankfurt/Main)

Breaks during the school day and other periods without lessons call for incentives for exercise, games activities and playing space. The schoolyard can also serve as the area for 'street games', inline skating, table tennis and for games with simple rules (Figure 4).

Figure 4: School yard (Landessportbund Hessen, Frankfurt/Main)

Swimming pools are particularly important for school sports. However, it is only worthwhile creating pools (even outdoor pools) in locations that are well served by the transport infrastructure. Best of all is the siting of a pool at the school location (Figure 5).

Figure 5: Indoor swimming pool (Helmut Blöcher, Kreuztal)

Requirements of Sport for All facilities

Until now, the 'classical' sports and their competition rules have almost exclusively dictated the requirements for facilities. This historical dominance has affected the provision of facilities for Sport for All.

With the expansion in sports activities in the 1980s and 1990s, the interests of those not so strongly interested in conventional sports, and not so clearly oriented to competitive sport, found greater consideration in the public debate. In the planning principles a sensible balance has genuinely been struck. There are already many facilities in which the co-existence of different sports, performance levels and groups of users function smoothly in practice.

This co-existence pre-supposes tolerance on the part of all interest groups and the correct social behaviour mentioned in the introduction, particularly in cases where compromises have to be made. A possible basic approach, serving a balance of interests, may involve responding accordingly to the proven present demand for conventional facilities, and systematically expanding the network of such sports facilities towards a greater leisure orientation. This will make it possible for conventional sports (soccer, gymnastics, athletics, for instance) to be supplemented by the so-called life-time sports of the 1970s and 1980s (swimming, table tennis, basketball, volleyball, tennis), and for today's trend sports (various forms of skating, streetball and beach sports) to also find their place in the activities offered to the population.

As in the preceding section, the term "multifunctionalism" is also applicable here.

Planning principles for facilities for joint use

It can generally be said today that the school sports curriculum is no longer the sole determining factor for the sports facilities provided in schools. In view of the social and leisure relevance of schools, the planning, construction and operation of sports facilities are of relatively far-reaching significance. The concept of sports education must also embrace the goal of social interaction.

Once the decision has been taken in favour of the joint use of sports facilities by schools, clubs and other interested sections of the population, it is advisable during town planning (or, in the case of smaller communities, inter-authority planning) to draw up a development plan laying down the guidelines for the joint planning of sports facilities and school buildings in the land use plan. This plan should also incorporate other play opportunities, youth welfare institutions, parks and gardens.

It is now, at the very latest, that *environmental concerns* have to be taken into consideration. In *'Bewegungsraum Stadt'* (*'The town as an exercise space'*), the authors Schemel and Strasdas formulate 'joint goals of sport and the environment in towns' and list the advantages for environmental quality, and for games and sport in their widest sense:

- Conservation of resources (land, energy)
- Protection and development of vacant inner-city spaces
- Protection from traffic-related air pollution and noise
- Enhancing the urban adventure quality
- Landscape conservation

Let us now turn to the *demand for facilities* (e.g. per class, per exercise group, per head of the population), which depends on:

- the popularity of the particular sport
- the available leisure time
- trends in school sports, with group or class size, approved school hours (ratio of optional to compulsory periods, activity groups), time-table (half-day or all-day schooling, block or individual periods)
- trends in club sport (size of club departments and of the overall clubs), and not least on
- trends in non-organized sports practised by the general public, taking account of the social structure in the planning district, acceptable travel distances to the facilities, and the cost to the individual user of practising their sport(s).

In the *choice of site* it should be borne in mind that schools are the most immobile users. Attempts should therefore be made to locate the required sports facilities on the school site or in the immediate neighbourhood.

In the *layout of the facility elements*, care should be taken to ensure that they could be used both separately and collectively. As many groups as possible (as well as different categories of users) should be able, without obstructing one another, to practise their sports simultaneously.

As to the *dimensioning and design of the facility elements*, the following points should be considered:

- In the design of sports facilities for primary schools, it is essential to give consideration to the age-related needs of their users, particularly with respect to the equipment.
- The facilities do not need to comply with the rules of the sports associations if the needs of the clubs concerned are fulfilled elsewhere.
- Demand from other groups, e.g. parents and children, certain disabled groups and for rehabilitation sport, can be catered for effectively at primary schools.

The basis for the planning and dimensioning of the individual facilities are the standards existing in most countries. Help is provided by the Basic Data for sports facilities published by the IAKS with financial support from the IOC.

Project planning

Project planning in the school sports sector depends on the number of sports periods per week, on morning or all-day school use, and on all-year or climate-related seasonal use. In the temperate climatic regions of Central Europe for instance, planning is based on three sports periods each per morning for 10 and a maximum of 12 classes with an average of 30 pupils. One exercise area in outdoor facilities and one in sports halls is required for this. When ascertaining demand, one or two periods of swimming are generally assumed for one age group only per week. On top of this there are activities available to the schools' interest and advanced groups in the early afternoon.

Sports facilities, and particularly outdoor ones, need to be skilfully integrated into their surroundings. A high-quality facility design, above and beyond functional requirements, enhances their appeal.

The basic provision of *outdoor facilities* should consist of heavy-duty small playing areas, grassed areas for gymnastics and small ball games, and athletic practice facilities (Figure 6). In primary schools the inclusion of a gymnastic play garden is recommended.

Figure 6: Optimal outdoor facilities (Helmut Blöcher, Kreuztal)

This range can be supplemented as required with large pitches and athletic training and competition facilities. In accordance with today's trends, opportunities for skateboarders, inline skaters and beach sports should also be provided.

In assessing the demand for *sports halls* the above-mentioned forms of use and modes of operation, of schools, clubs and other user groups must again be considered. The most sensible basic module for sports halls has proven to be 15 m x 27 m for gymnastics and small-area indoor games, including basketball for school lessons and Sport for All (Figure 7). The threefold of this basic module, the 27 m x 45 m hall, permits partition into three se- parate practice areas, or their combined use for indoor games requiring more space, and for competitive sport with limited spectator capacity (Figure 8).

Figure 7: Basic module for an indoor sport (Seiberth + Moser, CH-Arlesheim)

For primary schools, hall sizes of 10 m x 18 m and 12 m x 24 m are also possible as they are suitable for the less space-demanding games and sports of small children and the elderly. The most suitable size for bi-partite halls or pure ball game halls has proven to be 22 m x 44 m.

From the environmental point of view, only such construction materials should be used whose production and disposal does not pollute the environment. All conceivable economically feasible means of energy conservation, including energy recovery and the exploitation of solar energy, should be investigated.

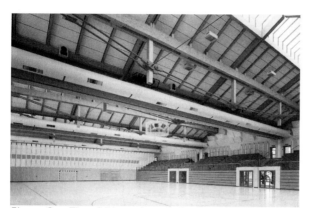

Figure 8:   Threefold version of the basic indoor sport hall module (Joseph Nordt, Kleinostheim)

Swimming pools are extremely attractive to schools and the general public. In view of the clear trend in swimming pool construction towards leisure-oriented bathing, parts of these pools should be assigned to joint school and club use, i.e. with swimming lane lengths of 25 m or 50 m outdoors or of 25 m in halls (Figure 9).

Figure 9:   Swimming pool construction appropriate for school and club use (Geller + Müller & Assoziierte, Euskirchen)

To serve all the user groups of a catchment area, an indoor pool must have a water area of about 450 m². Suitably divided, this area can be used for swimming lessons (8 m x 12.5 m), swimming, diving and water polo (12.5m x 25m). A water play area for 'parents and children' is essential (Figure 10).

Figure 10: Water play area (Hinke Schwimmbad Österreich GmbH, A-Vöcklamarkt)

A pool of this type does not, however, satisfy the growing trend towards leisure-oriented bathing in which fun elements can also be found. In connection with the non-swimmers' pool, these can consist of lazy rivers, underwater massage jets, bubble lounges, waterfalls and water slides, as well as saunas, artificial solariums and a cafeteria or restaurant (Figure 11).

Figure 11: A leisure-oriented swimming pool (Hinke Schwimmbad Österreich GmbH, A-Vöcklamarkt)

Outdoor pools can expect to attract a large number of visitors during periods of fine weather. Given an equally large planning district, a larger water area is required in addition to the games, sunbathing and rest areas. A tried-and-tested division of the 1,200 m² water area provides for a swimmers' pool (12.5 m x 25 m), a diving pool (12.5m x 12.5m), a non-swimmers'/fun pool covering 600 m², and a 'parents and children' area of about 100m² (Figure 12).

Figure 12: Outdoor swimming pool with attractions (Zeller Bäderbau GmbH, Berlin)

Swimming pools, and particularly indoor pools, require a considerable input of energy. Environmental measures as well make great economic sense as great environmental potential in terms of conserving resources and reducing pollution.

Organization of facility use, operation and maintenance

None of the facilities will operate smoothly in the long term without skilled management. This is a matter which has to be considered before the facility goes into operation.

For successful operation it is important for all the organizational issues to be handled by a single responsible department, with the involvement of all the user groups. The recruitment of suitable staff (in quality and quantity) is at the same time the basis for a high rate of capacity utilization.

Cost of construction, operation and maintenance

The choice of favourably located joint sites for schools and sports facilities, with the aid of the school development plan and the sports facility development plan, is also beneficial, amongst other things, to acceptable construction and operating costs. Even at the planning stage it is important to investigate in detail the effects of the structural concept, the selected design and the technical installations on maintenance and operating costs. If demand has been carefully analyzed it can be assumed that the facilities will be put to intensive use; the finish and equipment must therefore be hard-wearing and of high quality in order to keep maintenance and preservation costs to a minimum.

Summary

For a large number of the sports pursued in schools and as Sport for All, sports facilities are vital. Their provision helps to promote sports education and Sport for All. By combining these facilities and encouraging combined use, the pressure on building land, and on construction and operating costs is reduced whilst the rate of facility utilization is increased.

It is therefore imperative that all resources are pooled in convincingly affirming the importance of sport as essential to health and social behaviour if those responsible in politics and public administrations are to be convinced of the necessity to earmark sites and funds for the construction and operation of sports facilities.

Bibliography

Integration of facilities:

IAKS. (1972). Information meeting - Integration of sports centres and school premises – multi-functional facilities. *Sports Facilities and Swimming Pools*, 1, 137-184.

IAKS. (1973). Integration of sports centres and school premises - Results of working meetings. *Sports Facilities and Swimming Pools*, 1, 113-122.

IAKS. (1980). Integration of Sports Centres and School Premises - Utilization for school and club sports and non-organized leisure   groups. *IAKS Reference Series No. 11*, Cologne.

Chang, J.-H. (1999). Building a life-long Sport for All system in schools. *VII World Congress Sport for All, Congress Report*, Barcelona.

Hardman, K. (1999). Threats to school physical education! Threats to Sport for All. *VII World Congress Sport for All, Congress Report*, Barcelona.

Maglione, J.C. (1999). Education and sport: Symbiosis of hope for a better world. *VII World Congress Sport for All, Congress Report*, Barcelona.

Ziarrusta J.J. (1999). School Sport: Promoting a sporting lifestyle. *VII World Congress Sport for All, Congress Report*, Barcelona.

Environmental aspects:

Schemel H.-J., & Erbguth, W. (1992). *Handbuch Sport und Umwelt*. Aachen.

Chernushenko, D. (1994). *Greening our games - Running sports events and facilities that won't cost the earth*. Ottawa.

International Olympic Committee. (1995). *World conference on sport and the environment - Final report*. Lausanne.

The Lillehammer Conference - Forum on sport, environment and development. (1996). Lillehammer.

Da Costa, L.P. (1997). *Environment and sport - an international overview.* Porto.

International Olympic Committee. (1997). *Manual on sport and the environment.* Lausanne.

Schemel H.-J., & Strasdas, W. (1998). *Bewegungsraum Stadt - Bausteine zur Schaffung umweltfreundlicher Sport- und Spielgelegenheiten.* Aachen

Project planning:

IAKS. (1980). Planungsgrundlagen für den Bäderbau - Geltungsbereich für gemäßigte und kalte Klimazonen. *IAKS Reference Series No. 16.* Cologne.

IAKS. (1991). Sports Floors - IAKS Recommendations. *IAKS Reference Series No. 26.* Cologne.

IAKS. (1991). Planning Principles for Sports Halls. *IAKS Reference Series No. 29.* Cologne.

IAKS. (1992). Planning Guidelines Leisure Orientated Swimming Pools. *IAKS Reference Series No. 27.* Cologne, 1992

IAKS. (1993). Planning Principles for Sportsgrounds/Stadia. *IAKS Reference Series No. 33.* Cologne.

Perspectives, 1999, Vol. 1: 49-62
School Sport and Competition

SCHOOL SPORT AND COMPETITION: SPORTS MANAGEMENT

A European Approach to the Management of the Combination of Academics and Elite-Level Sport

Paul De Knop, Paul Wylleman, Jo Van Hoecke,
Kristine De Martelaer & Livin Bollaert

Scholastic Sport and Student-Athletes

The educational system, secondary (SE) and higher education (HE), has more and more been confronted with "competitive sport" as an "ever present cultural force" (Sobral, 1993). Due to the increased importance awarded to competitive, and more particularly to elite-level sport, academia did not only experience the need to provide its pupils (SE) or students (HE) the possibility to participate actively in competitions, but also to support those "student-athletes" who are actively involved in high-level sport outside of the educational setting. With the importance of the athletic achievements of these student-athletes in mind (e.g., at World University Games), as well as in view of the increasing interest for the social status of elite athletes--as exemplified in the International Olympic manifest which states clearly that an elite athlete must be provided with the best opportunities to develop a professional career (Olympic News, 1994)--it should not be surprising that nations try to optimise the situation of its student-athletes in order to nurse them on to higher levels of athletic achievements.

Reaching and remaining at a high competitive level requires talented athletes to participate in intensive and time-consuming training and competitions. In view of the development of athletes' athletic career, it is

Correspondence to: Prof. Dr. Paul De Knop, Gebouw L, Faculty of Physical Education and Physiotherapy, Vrije Universiteit Brussel, Pleinlaan 2, 1050 Brussels, Belgium evident that there is a large overlap with athletes' potential scholastic and academic career (Wylleman & De Knop, 1997a). Even if talented athletes do not go on to higher education, the basis of their sport career is developed concurrently with their scholastic involvement. While this need not be problematic, it does put talented athletes in a situation where they do need to invest their available time and energy into developing their potential in two areas of achievement.

Elementary in student-athletes' possibilities to combine an academic and athletic career is the establishment of a structural and organisational framework which allows academic institutes to accommodate the needs of their student-athletes (Wylleman, De Knop, Pluym, & Bogaerts, 1992; Wylleman, De Knop, & Theeboom, 1993). As such a framework or "student-athlete program" (SAP) needs to incorporate those services and personnel which facilitate student-athletes' combination of academic and athletic activities, and the managerial aspects need to be considered very carefully. It should therefore not be surprising that managing student-athletes' programs and (athletic) activities has been reported as being one of the larger and more significant sectors under the purview of sport management (Chelladurai & Riemer, 1997; De Knop, Wylleman, De Martelaer, Theeboom, & Wittock, 1996). It will be the role of the co-ordinator or sport manager to co-ordinate the resources, processes, and personnel in order to produce and exchange, in an efficient way, services which will enable student-athletes to achieve academic and athletic excellence in optimum circumstances. While generally acknowledged in North America, the role of the sport manager has up until now not yet been delineated in European student-athlete programs.

The current article aims therefore at describing the role sport managers can play in optimising student-athletes' efforts to combine academic and athletic activities. In order to integrate and facilitate the provision of services and personnel to student-athletes, managers need insight into the needs and wants of their "clientele". The relevance of managing the combination of academics and elite-level sport will therefore be introduced with an overview of the approach towards student-athletes taken at European level. Student-athletes' concrete needs and requirements will be described and situated within a framework, incorporating services and personnel, aimed at optimising the student-athletes' situation. In conclusion, aspects specific to the management of a student-athletes' program will be highlighted.

European Approach to Student-Athletes

While in North-America the status student-athletes hold is undeniable (Underwood, 1984; Whitford, 1990), in most European countries student-athletes' endeavours to excel at academic as well as athletic level has not gone untroubled. It is only during the past decade that initiatives have been developed in different European countries favouring the combination of academic and high-level athletic activities. In a comparative study, Wylleman and De Knop (1995a,b) provided an overview on the situation in 12 European countries. Results revealed that although in most countries the problems of student-athletes were not new, not all European countries have developed a positive climate in favour of their student-athletes. In those countries where no specific initiatives have as yet been developed, student-athletes are obliged to organise for themselves their studies as best as possible (e.g., appealing for support to the board of the school/university or to individual teachers/professors). The initiatives taken in order to optimise the situation of student-athletes can be situated on two axes, namely, a first axis related to the promoter of the initiative (i.e., academic or athletic governing bodies), and a second axis related to the localisation of the initiative (i.e., nationally or locally).

The majority of initiatives are realised in HE, due to, among others, their relative greater autonomy compared to the smaller sized secondary schools which are generally run within strict, centrally-dictated regulations. Institutes of HE are not only able to group more elite athletes, but are also more willing to invest (e.g., personnel, logistics) into a special student-athlete oriented initiative. Nevertheless, a distinct evolution was found to have taken place with regards to the initiatives in secondary level education: the specialised sports schools, which were nationally-centralised, are steadily replaced by de-centralised local initiatives, which provide guidance to young athletes in their own local schools. This evolution was not only due to organisational and financial problems (e.g., financing centralised full-time boarding schools), but also due to student-athletes' psycho-social problems (e.g., long periods away from home). Finally, results revealed that initiatives were generally developed by and within academic institutes, rather than by sports governing bodies (e.g., national Olympic Committee). In fact, central sports governing bodies were reported to show initially little interest in participating actively (e.g., financial support) in such initiatives.

The situation in France, Sweden and Belgium illustrate the diversity in approaches (see Figure 1).

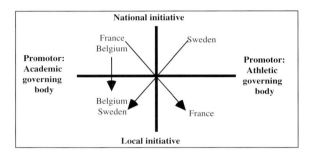

Figure 1: Diversity in managerial approaches to the combination of scholastic/academic and high-level competitive sport in different European countries (Wylleman & De Knop, 1995b).

France started with an initiative at national level by installing in 1974 the "Section Sport-Etudes" (SSE) at secondary education level. Each SSE aimed at guiding a group of 15-20 young talented athletes participating in the same sport within one secondary school. Each SSE was provided with (a) specialised coaches, (b) adequate sport equipment, (c) a boarding school, and (d) a co-ordinator ensuring the combination of study and sport. In 1984, 187 SSE regrouped 4321 young athletes in 26 different sport disciplines throughout France. However, due to, among others, a lack of adaptation of the study-system to the requirements of the young athletes, a lack of athletic achievements, and mediocre academic achievement rates, the SSE's were replaced in 1985 by the "Centres Permanent d'Entraînement et de Formation" (CPEF). Where the SSE were organized under the responsibility of the Ministry of Education within the existing frame-work of a local school, with admission criteria based on academic as well as athletic achievements, the CPEF are organized under the responsibility of the Ministry of Youth and Sports in function of the sport discipline (i.e., forming a network between local schools, universities, and industry) with admission only based on athletic achievements. The CPEF provide a specific flexibility in the study-organisation of their athletes by way of contracts with local schools and/or universities, specifying the concrete needs of these students. France evolved thus from a national, centralised approach, initiated within the academic environment, towards a de-centralised, sports-initiated approach.

Sweden started out also with a national initiative. At the beginning of the seventies the Swedish Sports Confederation initiated the "Sport Gymnasia" at secondary education level. Young athletes could adapt their school hours and time of study to the requirements of their athletic activities, while residing full-time in a boarding school. Its success led not only to an increase in the number of schools involved, but the Swedish parliament incorporated this system within the official educational system. 600 young athletes from 30 sport disciplines studied in some 60 schools in Sweden. However, due to psycho-social problems experienced by young athletes (e.g., home-sickness), a new initiative was introduced in 1983, namely, the "Local School Alternative", which permits young athletes to stay at home and to study in a local school, with flexible school hours. In this way Sweden established, parallel to a national sports-initiated approach, a local decentralised academic-initiated approach.

Finally, Belgium, and more specifically Flanders, witnessed the development of different types of initiatives during the past decade. At secondary education level, talented young athletes' possibilities to combine scholastic and high-level sport were very limited: only at the request of the sports federations, pupil-athletes could be granted flexibilities in a limited way (e.g., absence from school for international competitions). This changed drastically in 1998 when, on the initiative of the Flemish Ministry of Education, different schools throughout Flanders were granted the possibility to initiate a "topsport" subject of study for a limited number of sports (e.g., judo, tennis, volleyball, cycling). These schools are able to grant its pupil-athletes, among others, a curriculum including 20 hours general and 12 hours top-level sport per week, absence from school due to international competitions for a maximum of 60 days, high-level technical and physical training, and so forth. At higher education level, the Vrije Universiteit Brussel (VUB) grants since 1987 its elite student-athletes studying in one of its eight faculties specific academic flexibilities, as well as facilities at sports e.g., technical guidance, sports psychological guidance, sports physiotherapy, and logistic level e.g., housing on campus. This initiative was followed suit by other universities, and led to the organisation of an international colloquium on student-athletes (Wylleman, Schiltz, & Van Haeren, 1990) in consequence of which the Flemish Ministry of Education recognised officially the status of student-athletes in HE outside of university. While most initiatives were largely initiated by, and organised within, the educational setting, one particular approach involved the Belgian Olympic and Interfederal Committee and the Belgian Judo Federation to initiate a Olympic training centre on the campus of the Vrije Universiteit, Brussel. By centralising the training of its national team and talented judo-players on the university campus, it is able to provide boarding, as well as to co-operate with local schools (SE) and the VUB (HE) in order to provide flexibilities to its pupil-/student-athletes.

Specificity of Student-Athletes' Situation

The demands put on student-athletes to combine successfully an academic and an athletic career may lead them to experience problems on three levels.

On a *social level* student-athletes are confronted with the need to develop almost simultaneously two careers. As student-athletes have generally an amateur, or at best, a semi-professional status, they do not always have a sustainable income. The development of an academic career, leading up to a professional occupation, thus becomes inevitable during or after their athletic career (Wylleman & De Knop, 1997a). Problems occurring due to a lack of career management, or due to an overemphasis on one particular career, may have grave consequences for student-athletes on a social level. The type of education constitutes also an important social factor. For example, for "pupil-athletes" in SE the consequences of compulsory attendance is the most important problem, more particularly the restricted possibility to train and/or compete (Wylleman, De Knop, Pluym, & Bogaerts, 1992). In contrast, student-athletes in HE are required to be more personally involved in developing their academic career: the relative high degree of freedom at college or university requires from student-athletes a stronger need to attend academic activities e.g., relative long examination periods, and a more systematic planning of their study-activities e.g., preparation for exams--a personal involvement which is not always readily forthcoming, or which is obstructed by those in their immediate surrounding e.g., coach.

Taking these social requirements into account, it should not be surprising that student-athletes are heavily dependent upon their *psycho-social environment* in order to combine successfully academic and athletic demands (Wylleman & De Knop, 1996). For example, research revealed elite student-athletes to rate the support provided by the academic institute, the coach and the parents as most influential in being able to succeed in both careers--support ranging from informational, financial or logistic, to emotional in nature (Wylleman & De Knop, 1997b). At the psycho-social level the role of the peer group is also important: a lack of time may lead student-athletes to have under-developed relationship skills, and thus, restricted, or even distorted, peer group relationships and development of the self-concept.

The demands and problems occurring at a (psycho-)social level may finally lead to the occurrence of problems at an *individual/personal level*, such as lack of self-confidence or motivation, lack of academic skills, or problems with time-management. It is important to note that student-athletes do expect for themselves, and are expected by their psychological environment, to go to the limit of their capabilities in developing not only their academic and athletic careers, but also their personal lives e.g., familial, relationships. Participating in intensive and time-consuming training and competitions, in academic e.g., colleges, and in daily e.g., recuperation, relaxation activities, requires them therefore to adhere conscientiously to minutely daily planning. This may confront student-athletes with time-management concerns, stress-related problems, developmental obstacles e.g., coping with failure, and so forth. On an academic level, setting time aside to study or to attend lectures does not guarantee that student-athletes have the academic skills required to study adequately during the time allowed. A study comparing the adherence to academic activities of student-athletes with that of students involved in "other-than-academic activities" e.g., fraternity, revealed student-athletes to report more academic problems caused by lack of time and physical fatigue due to their sports involvement than did the other students (Wylleman, De Knop, & Theeboom, 1993). Nevertheless, student-athletes devoted the same amount of time to their studies, but invested more time to their athletic activities than did the other students to their "other-than-academic activities".

It is important to realise that student-athletes are confronted, be it in SE or in HE, with a number of situations, and with an environment, which could lead them to experience a number of problems at different levels. While these problems are not restricted to student-athletes alone i.e., other students or other athletes are also confronted with some of these problems, its uniqueness lies in the fact that student-athletes do actually run a great risk of experiencing all these problems simultaneously. The management of a student-athlete program will therefore need to identify the services and personnel which can support student-athletes in preparing for, and tackling effectively these problems.

Establishing and Managing a Student-Athlete Program

In order to plan, initiate, lead, develop, and evaluate a Student-Athlete Program (SAP), the manager will in first instance need to establish the operative goal of the SAP (Slack, 1997). In view of the specificity of the European context e.g., no traditional link between educational and athletic world, low profile of interscholastic/intercollegiate sports, it is important to acknowledge that such an operative goal will differ quite thoroughly from that of North American intercollegiate athletics (Chelladurai & Danylchuk, 1984). A SAP needs to have as its operative goal the efficient and effective provision of services and personnel that enable pupil/student-athletes to succeed at academic and athletic level, while taking into account their developmental needs. It should be clear that a SAP is in essence an organisation that enables its pupil/student-athletes to develop their talent within the framework of their own personal development, rather than that of the educational institute's prestige or public relations. The European context also entails that a SAP takes an academic rather than an athletic perspective. Although, for example, in Canada the functions of public relations and prestige can be considered as a top objective of intercollegiate athletics (Chelladurai & Danylchuk, 1984), it is deemed that this is not the case in most European countries. The manager needs therefore to ensure that the governance of the educational setting--be it locally e.g., school board, chancellor or nationally e.g., Ministry of Education--not only accept the *need* to establish a SAP, but is also willing to provide the *support* required e.g., financial, logistic, personnel, to initiate and run the SAP successfully. Establishing the need for a SAP should be based upon a detailed description of the size and specificity of the pupil/student-athlete population vis-à-vis the total pupil/student population, and thus address the question of why it is justified to (re-)direct funds and personnel to this particular group of pupils/students. An approach particularly poignant for most European countries consists of focusing on pupil/student-athletes striving towards academic excellence--not as a determinant of athletic eligibility, but in view of academic progress and success. For example, in Flanders (Belgium) young talented athletes were not able to actively combine academia and athletics in higher education (Wylleman, De Knop, & Theeboom, 1993). Several of these talented athletes chose to join a US-based university in order to further their athletic excellence. This changed in 1987 when the Vrije Universiteit Brussel (VUB) initiated its Department of Top-level Sport and Study (DTS). It was founded on the basis of the "principle of equality": talented youngsters should be able to achieve academic and athletic excellence in one and the same period of life without having to go abroad to study. This emphasis not only led student-athletes to be recognised as a "target-group" among other students (rather than as "athletes" on campus), but also established the DTS as an "academic" rather than as an "athletic" department within the university. This academic perspective, strengthened by the fact that the head of the DTS is a professor and thus a full-member of the academic staff of the university, revealed to be an asset when academia-related services e.g., rescheduling exams, tutoring had to be installed and developed within the university.

While a SAP will generally be supported initially and to some extent by the educational setting e.g., personnel, the need for external funding e.g., sponsoring, will also come about. It is at this time that a SAP's primary goal, which is academic in nature, could be seen as a "restriction": more particularly, potential sponsors can be reluctant in acknowledging academic excellence as a valuable "return" for their support. An alternative to sponsoring can be found in establishing the SAP in an extra-mural network involving governmental and non-governmental partners related to academic and athletic excellence e.g., Ministry of Education, national Olympic committee, sport federation.

In the second instance, the SAP-manager needs to identify pupil/student-athletes' requirements in the academic, athletic, and personal realms, and provide those services which will provide pupil/student-athletes (a) with a smooth entry into school or campus-life when starting the combination at SE or HE-level, (b) an optimal combination during their academic career, and (c) an efficient transition from being a pupil/student-athlete after finalising their SE or HE education. Those services will generally include academic monitoring, tutoring, and planning e.g., developing study skills and time management skills; access to athletic infrastructure and guidance e.g., assistant-coach; guidance with regard to the development and optimising of life-skills e.g., relationship skills, stress-management; and logistic support e.g., on-campus housing. In order to provide some of these services, the manager will need to consider working with specialists in the fields of academia e.g., tutor, athletics e.g., physical educator, and personal development e.g., sport psychologist. These specialists may consult on a one-to-one basis, or within specific workshops or programs.

Finally, the manager will need to identify the SAP's organisational goal(s) which will provide guidelines regarding decision making, appraisal of effectiveness, evaluation of services and personnel, and so forth. Integration of the SAP within the educational setting, utilisation patterns by pupil/student-athletes, administrative and logistic efficiency and effectiveness, intra- and extra-mural rapport-building e.g., teachers, faculty members, partners, are but some of the factors which will be part of the evaluation of a SAP. However, in the end, the final evaluation criteria should be the rate of academic success of pupil/student-athletes. To what extent are pupil/student-athletes able to succeed academically in the subject of study of their choice and within an acceptable period of time, while maintaining or enhancing their level of athletic achievements? While many of its student-athletes have performed at Olympic or World level, De Knop and Wylleman (1998) deem the real measure of success of the DST to be the student-athletes' rate of academic success which is ten percent higher than that of the total student population.

Conclusions

Elementary to the success of student-athletes is establishing a structural and organisational framework, such as a SAP, which allows academic institutes to accommodate the needs of its student-athletes. Central to the installation and management of such a framework is the role of the SAP-manager who will manage the current resources, processes and personnel, so that the student-athletes can strive for academic and athletic excellence in optimal circumstances. In order to be effective and efficient in providing services to this public, a SAP manager will need to identify the orienting goals which will provide guidelines for decision making, appraisal of effectiveness, and so on. The manager will also need to identify the needs and requirements of his/her target group so he/she can determine the specific services which have to be delivered. Finally, the co-ordinator will need to evaluate the effectiveness of the program in accordance to its defined mission and derived operative goals. Central to this task will be the surveying of the present field of operations, evaluating existing policy with a view to spotting problems, and exploring possibilities for further development.

The combination of scholastic/academic and high-level sport is a specific problem within educational settings. It requires from pupil/student-athletes various individual related capabilities to achieve excellence at both levels, whilst keeping in balance their personal development. However, as the managerial aspects of realising such a combination are put up front, it becomes evident that not only the educational setting, but also the world of sports, need to take up their responsibility. Furthermore, and especially at European level, the need for collaboration, via exchange of information and co-operation, may be beneficiary to the guidance of student-athletes within each country. In order to enhance such a pan-European co-operation, empirical and applied data on the specificity, as well as generalisability of the situation of pupil/student-athletes in different countries, should be gathered and compared.

Due to the general nature of the recommendations outlined earlier, no best solution for student-athletes in all possible situations may be guaranteed. However, it is hoped that this paper may provide an initial basis for recognising, approaching and *managing* the specific situation of student-athletes in Europe.

References

Chelladurai, P., & Danylchuk, K.E. (1984). Operative goals of intercollegiate athletics: Perceptions of athletic administrators. *Canadian Journal of Applied Sport Sciences*, **9**, 33-41.

Chelladurai, P., & Riemer, H.A. (1997). A classification of facets of athlete satisfaction, *Journal of Sport Management*, **11**, 133-159.

De Knop, P., & Wylleman, P. (1998*). 10 Jaar Topsport en Studie [10 Years Topsport and Study]* (p. 1). Brussel, Belgium: Vrije Universiteit Brussel.

De Knop, P., Wylleman, P., De Martelaer, K., Theeboom, M., & Wittock, H. (1996). New management for university sport, *European Journal for Sport Management*, **3** (1), 35-47.

Olympic News (December, 1994). *De 61 aanbevelingen en conclusies van het IOC Conges [The 61 recommendations and conclusions of the IOC Congress]*, 11-12.

Slack, T. (1997). *Understanding sport organizations. The application of organization theory*. Champaign, IL: Human Kinetics.

Sobral, F. (1993). Psychological outcomes of school sport: A non-psychologist's view. In S. Serpa, J. Alves, V.Ferreira, & A. Paula-Brito (Eds.), *Proceedings of the 8th World Congress Sport Psychology* (pp. 146-153). Lisboa, Portugal: Universidade Técnica de Lisboa.

Underwood, C. (1984). *The student athlete: Eligibility and academic integrity*. East-Lansing, MI: Michigan State University Press.

Withford, D. (1990). The student athlete: Myth or reality?, *College Magazine*, **2**, 37-41.

Wylleman, P., & De Knop, P. (1995a). *Athlètes de haut niveau et enseignement: perspective Européenne sur la combinaison d'etude et sport de haut niveau (High-level athletes and education: European perspective on the combination of study and high-level sport)*. Paper presented at the Congres d'Etude et Sport (Congress Study and Sport), Montréal, Canada: Université de Montréal-Ecole de Mortagne, 27- 29.01.95.

Wylleman, P., & De Knop, P. (1995b). *The influence of the social network on young student-athletes*. Paper presented at the International Congress on Physical Education and Sport of Children, Bratislava, Slovakia: FIEP, 13-16.08.95.

Wylleman, P. & De Knop, P. (1996). *Combining academic and athletic excellence: The case of elite student-athletes*. Paper presented at the International Conference of the European Council for High Ability "Creativity and Culture", Vienna, Austria: ECHA, 19-22.10.96.

Wylleman, P., & De Knop, P. (1997a). *Elite student-athletes: Issues related to career development and social support*. Paper presented at the 12th Annual Conference on Counselling Athletes, Springfield, US: Springfield College, 29.05-01.06.97.

Wylleman, P., & De Knop, P. (1997b). The role and influence of the psycho-social environment on the career transitions of student-athletes. In Bangsbo et al. (Eds.), *Book of abstracts 2nd Annual Congress of the European College of Sports Science* (pp. 90-91). Copenhagen: University of Copenhagen.

Wylleman, P., De Knop, P., & Theeboom, M. (1993). *Academic problems and achievements of elite athletes at university (Elite athletes in higher education)*. Paper presented at the FISU/CESU-Conference van de XVII Universiade, Bufallo, United States: University at Bufallo, 09-11.07.93.

Wylleman, P., De Knop, P., De Martelaer, K., & Teyrlinck, P. (1991). Combining top level sport and university studies: problems, possible solutions and the need for an international perspective. In *Proceedings XVI Universiade - FISU/CESU-Conference*, Sheffield City Polytechnic.

Wylleman, P., De Knop, P., Pluym, T., & Bogaerts, K. (1992). The top-level athlete in secondary and higher education in Flanders. In UNISPORT (Ed.), *Proceedings Olympic Scientific Congress - Vol. 2* (p. PED 103). Malaga, Spain: Unisport.

Wylleman, P., Schiltz, G., & Vanhaeren, N. (1990). *Proceedings International Symposium 'Top-level sport and Study'*. Brussels, Belgium: BLOSO-VBT/VUSF.

Perspectives, 1999, Vol. 1: 63-72
School Sport and Competition

SCHOOL SPORT AND COMPETITION: SPORTS PEDAGOGY

Examples from Germany

Herbert Haag

Introduction

The given topic has two main aspects:
a. Competitive sport (including training) at different levels of performance.
b. School sport with different content dimensions.

These two aspects also constitute in reality a mix of both. This mix, however, is realized in many different socio-cultural variations. This again provides for a huge number of examples, models, and approaches to competition in school sport. This wide variety cannot be analyzed within the framework of one paper. Therefore this contribution – written from the point of view of pedagogical perspectives – is based on examples from one country: Germany.

In order to include descriptions and statements which have a certain degree of external and internal validity, data from the following two dictionaries in English for the field of sport, sport education, and sport science have been used in this article:

- Beyer, E. (Ed.) (1987). *Dictionary of Sport Science. German, English, French*. Schorndorf: Hofmann.
- Haag, G. & Haag, H. (Eds.) (1999). *Dictionary for Sport and Sport Science* (in print).

Correspondence to: Professor Dr. Herbert Haag, Institut für Sport und Sportwissenschaften, Christian-Albrechts-Universität, Kiel, Olshausenstr. 74, 24098 Kiel, Germany.

The dictionary of Schabel & Thieß (1993) is not used in this context. It offers, however, valuable additional information on the given topic.

Following a short introduction relative to the basic components of this topic the following three examples from present day Germany will be presented:
- Deutsches Sportabzeichen (German Sports Badge).
- Bundesjugendspiele (Federal Youth Games).
- Jugend trainiert für Olympia (Youth training for the Olympics).

Finally, a short analysis of the pedagogical perspectives within the mix of competition and school sport will be presented.

Competition (sportive) – Competitive Sport

For a general meaning competition is a "term for a comparison of sportive performances, which is characterized by the following elements: equality of opportunities, ordered organization which is prescribed in the rules, sanctions for rule violations, spiritual (experience of participation), symbolic (prestige, winning of a medal or cup) or material (prize) value. The origins of sport competitions are generally regarded to lie in Greek agonistics and athletics. Modern forms of sport competitions are, on the one hand, justified by the arguments of goal orientation, adventure, etc.; on the other hand, they are also subjected to strong criticism (critical sport theory). Sport competitions are closely related to training (testing), which must be viewed as a prerequisite for a pedagogically responsible competition. The term competition is also used for an athlete's rival(s) in a certain sport event" (Haag & Haag 1999, 100).

Quite often the paradigm of competition is used for the teaching and learning process in the so-called competitive form. This means "sportive exercising in the form of a competition; in addition to play form and basic form, it represents one of the three fundamental exercise forms which make the realization of motor learning possible. The competitive form is utilized when a general pool of motor abilities has already been established through play and basic form. The advantage of the competitive form lies in the generally higher motivation for exercising. A disadvantage is that the idea of competition leads to inadequate movement execution in some cases. The competitive form has an important function in the preparation for competition" (Haag & Haag 1999, 100).

There are many types or forms of sport in general. One can also say that sport has many "faces". Therefore dealing with sport as one large social sub-system of almost every – mainly industrialized – society, one has to differentiate and see various dimensions of sport. One very important dimension is competitive sport. This is a "form of sport prevalent in competition with the goal of delivering the highest possible personal performance. Competitive sport in a narrower sense is high-performance sport, or top-level sport, when performance is understood as absolute performance. This form of sport requires a very high level of technical and personal effort in order to get as close as possible to the pre-set norms e.g., record, championship or to set new norms. To achieve this the following are necessary: planned performance promotion as it is undertaken within the framework of talent promotion in high-performance centres, specialization, and systematic training (also high-performance training) for participation in competitive sport. In a broader sense competitive sport (performance sport, when performance is understood as relative performance) represents all sport activity, since sport and performance are inseparable. The important point in this interpretation is that the athlete determines the demand level of his competitive (performance) sport for himself. Similar to performance and the performance principle and depending thereupon, competitive sport in a narrower sense has been controversially discussed in sport and social sciences (also critical theory). In order to confront effectively the indisputable dangers associated with competitive sport, e.g. physical damage caused by early intensive specialized training, devaluation of sport to a stabilizing factor of societal and/or economic systems, etc., competitive sport represents a thematic focus of sport science as a whole and of individual scientific institutes" (Haag & Haag, 1999, 100-101).

In summary the terms competition, competitive form, and competitive sport can provide a sound theoretical framework for the topic to be analyzed.

Physical Education – School Sport

The paradigm of competition can also be linked to the concrete procedure of physical education, predominantly realized within school sport. Both concepts are linked closely to each other.

Physical education (P.E.) is "education through the body which can be seen as an encompassing complement to intellectual training within the total educational system. It stands in contrast to the traditional gymnastics programme which aimed mainly at the acquisition of skills. The objectives of P.E. in schools are defined as movement education, health education, play education. From the perspective of an anthropologically based theory of education, P.E. strives for the development and formation of human beings who experience their corporality in an existential way both as access to the physical world and to social communication. The significance of P.E. for basic education is exhibited by the didactics of physical education.

To formulate the educational mission, the basic term "body" (Leib), also used in the area of cultural anthropology, is used to guard against a materialistic interpretation e.g., physical culture. This basic term is outdated and could lead one to view the mind as the opposite pole of the body and thus evoke old-fashioned dualistic conceptions.

A complete theory of P.E. was formulated in the Federal Republic of Germany only after World War II. In the 1960s the emphasis was on didactic "principles" e.g. developmental approach, naturalness, holistic, spontaneity, etc. Latterly, P.E.'s narrow link with the school system has been loosened and extracurricular sport has been given more consideration, the spectrum of the scientific foundation of P.E. has expanded as well. In this way a complex theory has developed which, among others, includes sociological considerations and scientific concepts of training.

Within the system of sport science, the theory of P.E. is currently represented by the discipline of sport pedagogy. For the lack of a synonym, the term P.E. remains indispensable for the description of educational intentions and processes (based on Bernett in Beyer 1987, 369-371).

On the basis of this concept of physical education comments on school sport can be better understood, namely as physical exercises, meaning the "totality of all forms of sport activity at all types and levels of schools, either as mandatory or instructional school sport, or as voluntary or extracurricular school sport e.g., training groups, sport competitions and festivals. The concepts for guidelines and curricula for school sports are provided by public sport administration. Furthermore, sport self-administration is also concerned with foundations, methods, contents, supplementary, advanced or enhancing measures; non-school federations and interest groups on state or national levels support these efforts. Sport science discusses issues related to school sport predominantly in the disciplines of sport didactics and sport pedagogy. The reality of school sport was characterized for a long time as the "misery of school sport", a consequence of the focus on the mental contents and theoretical concepts in school instruction. Even though a positive trend can be observed currently towards a more comprehensive interpretation of sport, and therefore also of school sport, a deep gap still remains between school sport and sport outside of schools" (Haag & Haag 1999, 367).

It has to be pointed out, however, despite a given connection between competition and school sport, that there is a fundamental difference between the German, almost European, and the North-American approach to this issue. In the German school system competition only plays a minor role, mainly geared towards sport for all competition; the competitive sport for children and youth is predominantly carried out in very strong and specialized sport clubs. In contrast to this sport is included within the school system (all day school –comprehensive high school) in North America in a much broader sense since there is no club system comparable to Europe available. This essential difference has to be observed in dealing with the subject of this paper. Examples from Germany, which will follow, mainly relate to competition in the form of sport for all.

Deutsches Sportabzeichen (German Sports Badge)

This German Sports Badge (Haag 1987, 114, 116) was introduced by Prof. Dr. Carl Diem (1882-1962) in 1912 (since 1921 also for women) according to a pattern used in Sweden. Today this badge is sponsored by the German Sports Federation and awarded for a variable performance ability in sport. Since 1958 it is also recognized as a State Honour Award. Within one year men and women have to choose one discipline out of each of five groups of disciplines, different for men and women. Further elective disciplines are available. The badge is given in three classes: bronze, silver, and gold. A special gold award is given for successful repetition in five consecutive years. There is also a variation of the requirements for getting the badge by persons with disabilities. Two variations for the German Sports Badge in school sport are of central importance:

German Sports Badge for Pupils

This has been awarded since 1969 by the German Sports Federation for multi-dimensional performance ability in sport by pupils aged 8-12. There are again five groups of disciplines of which one discipline has to be chosen out of four groups, mainly of track and field events; swimming is always required as one discipline. Additional gymnastics disciplines can be chosen. There are three classes: bronze 8-10, silver 11-12, and gold after one repetition.

German Sports Badge for Youth

This has been awarded since 1925 for boys, and since 1927 for girls; today it is sponsored by the German Sports Federation. It has the same pattern as for adults or pupils, apart from offering different disciplines and requirements (five groups of disciplines and additional elective disciplines). It is awarded in four classes: bronze (13-14), bronze with silver (15-16), silver (17), and gold, if all classes are awarded with at least two repetitions. There is also a special plan for handicapped youth.

In a time of internationalization and globalization it is also interesting that there is a "European Youth Sports Badge" for the ages 16-18. The "German Sports Badge for Youth" in silver can be transferred into the "European Youth Sports Badge".

Bundesjugendspiele (Federal Youth Games)

These competitions were introduced in 1951 in the schools of the former Federal Republic of Germany (Becker in Röthig 1992, 99-100). The equivalent was the "Kinder- und Jugendspartakiade" of the former "German Democratic Republic" (until 1989). There is a governing board for the "Federal Youth Games" with representatives from the State Ministers of Culture, the Federal Government and the German Sports Federation.

These games aim to promote an interest in sport, especially in competitive sport. The disciplines related to track and field originally and were enlarged to include swimming and gymnastics. Within the chosen sport a triathlon has to be performed. Since 1979 schools with compulsory physical education classes have to arrange these "Federal Youth Games" yearly, and participation in this "Federal Youth Games" is compulsory from grade 3 to 10. The conference of the State Ministers for Culture announces the framework of the "Federal Youth Games" for every year. Within this framework the schools can carry out their own version of the "Federal Youth Games". They are performed within one day and should be supported by a school sport festival. The results are honoured with a victory or honour diploma, and can be used in calculating a grade in physical education given at the end of the school year. The results also can count towards fulfilling the requirements for the "German Sports Badge for Pupils", or the "German Sports Badge for Youth".

The "Federal Youth Games" had several predecessors in history. From 1920-1933 the "Reichsjugendwettkämpfe" for boys and girls (10-18) took place always on August 11, the date on which the Weimar constitution was adopted in 1919. The "Deutsche Reichsausschuß für Leibesübungen" organized these Games. From 1934-1936 the "Reichserziehungs-ministerium" organized the "Deutsches Jugendsportfest". In 1937 this form of the festival was changed to the "Reichssportwettkampf der HJ" – a clearly national-socialist oriented undertaking.

Thus it can be seen, that these sport-for-all oriented competitions in school sport have a long tradition in Germany, unfortunately abused from 1933-1945 (also later in the GDR); however, from 1951 until today the "Federal Youth Games" can be seen as a valuable part of school sport in Germany.

Jugend trainiert für Olympia (Youth Training for the Olympics)

This competitive event was introduced in 1969 as a sporting competition for school sport teams in the former Federal Republic of Germany. In the most popular school sport disciplines selection competitions are organized in 3 to 4 classes at regional and state level. The teams which win at state level participate in the spring and autumn in the final competitive tournament held always in Berlin. The finals for the winter sports are held alternatively in the state of Bavaria, Baden-Württemberg, or Lower Saxonia.

It was decided that competition would be in team sports and not in dual or individual sports. The reason for this is that within victory or defeat in team sports the individual pupils or students are not alone. Therefore this competition in sport is, from an educational point of view, better and is more sound with regard to the mental attitude of the young competitors.

Pedagogical Perspectives for Competition in School Sport

Competition in sport is based on the paradigm of equal opportunity within a set of rules, for individuals, groups (teams), or nations competing for an ideal, symbolic or material value (Hagedorn in Röthig 1992, 557-559).

The ideal nature of competition is related to the experience of working together or against each other, as well as to performance comparison in winning or being defeated on the basis of rules (constitutive – and regulative). The symbolic nature of competition is seen when the process and product (result) of competition gains a special meaning e.g. repetition of archaic patterns; catharsis; reversibility of the reality; personal or political prestige. The material nature of competition is almost solely focused on the result, as well as the product or victory, and it includes personal gifts, awards, money etc.

It is quite understandable that the pedagogical or educational value of competition in school sport is mainly seen in the ideal and symbolic nature of competition. The educational value is mainly connected to competition, being one avenue for children and youth to show performance, and by this to create something that has value for the development of self-image, self-consciousness and self-esteem (Mechling 1989). This performance then can be evaluated in five dimensions: evaluation with oneself, within the peer group, with other similar groups, with relative norms e.g. percentile norms and absolute norms e.g. world records. Again it is quite clear that, from self-evaluation to evaluation with absolute norms, the pedagogical-educational value is constantly diminished.

It can be seen as a valid assumption that it is an anthropological pattern that human beings want to perform. In this regard especially school sport offers a chance for children and youth to have valuable life experiences by engaging in training for competitive sport (Carl 1987), and by competing in sport as offered within the framework of the school system. This has been analyzed, drawing on examples from Germany, by describing their three forms of competition in school sport.

Concluding Comments

If one agrees that the major aim of schooling is to prepare children and youth for life as adults in an ever changing society, then it is legitimate to include competition in school sport. The word sport by its nature includes the notion of performing, competing, and comparing the performance shown in a competition by evaluation.

The fact that competition in top-level athletics is facing many often negative developments, which are more akin to the world of business and professional life, cannot diminish the original educational value of competition in school sport as outlined in this analysis. Certain volumes of the book series of the International Council of Sport Science and Physical Education (ICSSPE), with the name "Sport Science Studies", prove that the issue of the development of sport in the context of overall social development, especially in the form of competitive sport at all levels, is of high value. In this connection I refer to volume 3 "The Search for Sporting Excellence" (Fisher & Borms 1990), volume 7, "Sport in a Changing Society" (Digel 1995), and volume 10 "Physical Activity and Active Lifestyle of Children and Youth" (Naul, Hardman, Piéron & Skirstad 1998). In all three volumes contributions relate to the topic of competition in school sport, thus offering a further source for related research based information.

References

Beyer, E. (Ed.) (1987). *Dictionary of Sport Science. German, English, French*. Schorndorf: Hofmann.

Carl, K. (1989). Trainingswissenschaft – Trainingslehre. In H. Haag, B. Strauß & S. Heinze (Red.), *Theorie- und Themenfelder der Sportwissenschaft* (pp. 216-228). Schorndorf: Hofmann.

Digel, H. (1995). *Sport in a Changing Society. Sociological Essays*. Schorndorf: Hofmann.

Fisher, R.J. & Borms, J. (1990). *The Search for Sporting Excellence*. Schorndorf: Hofmann.

Haag, H. (Red.). (1987) *Schüler-Duden Sport*. Mannheim: Dudenverlag.

Haag, G. & Haag, H. (Eds.) (1999). *Dictionary for Sport and Sport Science* (in print).

Mechling, H. (1989). Leistung und Leistungsfähigkeit im Sport. In H. Haag, B. Strauß & S. Heinze (Red.), *Theorie- und Themenfelder der Sportwissenschaft* (pp. 230-251). Schorndorf: Hofmann.

Naul, R., Hardman, K., Piéron, M. & Skirstad, B. (Eds.) (1998). *Physical Activity and Active Lifestyle of Children and Youth*. Schorndorf:Hofmann.

Röthig, P. (Red.) (1992) *Sportwissenschaftliches Lexikon*. Schorndorf: Hofmann.

Schnabel, G. & Thieß, G. (Hrsg.) (1993). *Lexikon Sportwissenschaft. Leistung – Training- Wettkampf. Band I und II*. Berlin: Sportverlag.

Non-Specialist Bibliography

Budinger, H. & Hahn, E. (1990).   Bedingungen des sportlichen Wettkampfes. Schorndorf: Hofmann.

Kuhlmann, D. (1999).   Wettkampfsport: Domäne in der Defensive? Theoretische Ansätze und empirische Befunde. Schorndorf: Hofmann.

Perspectives, 1999, Vol. 1: 73-83
School Sport and Competition

SCHOOL SPORT AND COMPETITION: SPORTS PEDAGOGY

Roland Naul

Problems

The world-wide analysis of the position and development of Physical Education in the nineties showed that the 'Golden Period' of the seventies is long gone - many countries are employing fewer Physical Education teachers and spending less money on school sport facilities and their maintenance.

While these external changes have been taking place, internal changes have also occurred. However, in contradiction to the general reduction (number of classes conducted, number of employed Physical Education teachers, financial resources, etc.), the internal changes increased the educational requirements and pedagogical ambitions of traditional Physical Education. These extensions and additions can be described as follows: Movement Education, Health Education, Security (Safety) Education, Environmental Education, Intercultural Education, and Ethics. This list includes only some of the requirements which are emphasised in Physical Education today. Sport Pedagogy and Physical Education have had to meet these and other new pedagogical requirements during the past twenty years. Meanwhile, traditional aims, tasks and educational values of Physical Education have been reduced, rolled back, or even cancelled.

Correspondence to: Professor Dr. Roland Naul, Universität Essen, FB2, Sportpädagogik, Ellernstr. 31, 4300 Essen 12, Germany.

This internal change to Physical Education is most impressive considering the principal aim and objective of Physical Education throughout many decades: competition. Hardly any other objective in Physical Education is as controversial as high level performance and competition. While some Physical Education teachers expect a negative influence on their students when emphasising efficiency and performance, others regard this as a main means of influencing the personality in a positive way.

In many countries external and internal changes in Physical Education during the last twenty years have led to a new definition and discussion concerning the tasks and objectives of Physical Education. This applies to the argument concerning the need to retain traditional tasks and objectives alongside the introduction of new aims and roles. In the discussions between traditionalists and reformers about tasks and objectives, efficiency and performance have been critical points because competition and fun are considered contradictory or incompatible.

Perspective

This and some other controversies about aims and objectives of modern Physical Education appear in a different perspective if the external changes i.e. changes in politics, in society, and in social structures, and the internal changes i.e. personnel, educational, and interactive changes, are considered dialectically and not separately. Such consideration from a multiperspective point of view, encompassing the whole process of change and all interrelated influences on Physical Education, offers a new viewpoint on the controversy about the strengths and weaknesses of performance as a principal aim.

On the one hand, performance historically reached a status of independence and nearly lost its pedagogical substance during the social process of differentiation and definition of sport. On the other hand, an educational understanding of Physical Education has developed and diversified, which largely ignores athletic performance as an educational aim, doubts its educational potential, and only recognises it as a negative influence.

Both lines of development: the de-pedagogical transfer of the idea of competition, and the non-athletic objective of education in Physical

Education, need to be corrected and have to be unified in a new common perspective for the future.

But what are the reasons, and where are the sources for this noticeable divergence of the athletic and educational elements of Physical Education?

The Roots of the Past

First of all we have to keep in mind that in the first modern educational element of Physical Education in schools is the idea of the development of physical achievement. Continuous improvement and testing of this physical achievement during classes was integrated and regarded as an educational task. Johann Christoph Fiedrich Gutsmuths described and explained this very thoroughly in his book "Gymnastik für die Jugend", which is internationally well-known and was translated into all important languages in the 19th century.

At the time when Guthsmuths recorded his objectives and aims of Physical Education in 1793, there was no sport in schools. He referred to Physical Education and sport as exercises, as illustrated in the title of his book. Even in the mother country of sport, the English Public Schools, neither athletics nor games were known as school sports at this early time. The educational objectives of introducing athletics and sport into Public Schools were written down some decades later. Guthsmuths called it educational exercises, composed mostly of running, jumping, throwing, swimming and ice-skating, but also including exercises such as climbing and balancing. The measure for the physical performance shown was individualised for each student, showing individual development and improvement in performance, for example in long jump or high jump, during the school year. Guthsmuths wrote the results down and kept the scores of each individual student. The performance achieved by the individual student was published in a school 'Score-Table' in the school building. The requirement for 'achievement', and the development of 'achievement', in Physical Education in schools are neither a phenomenon of modern sport nor a characteristic that is connected with sport directly.

According to Guthsmuths, competition was a basis and required a pedagogical element for learning in school, and for the future development of the students' personality. At that time they had no 'athletic records' with which to compare the students' achievements objectively. But even if they had had such external measures for an objective assessment of the physical achievement of the students, the application of such measures for the assessment of the students' achievement would have been contradictory to Guthsmuths' pedagogical principles of education. He emphasised an individualised, harmonious and holistic education for his students.

These pedagogical principles from Guthsmuths' theory were retained even during the second half of the 20th Century when athletics and games were already a generally accepted means of education in the Public Schools of Victorian and Edwardian times. Physical achievement, compared individually in athletics and between teams such as rowing and football, was considered a valuable means of forming character. Physical educators and teachers of many European countries visited English Public Schools, were enthusiastic about this new spirit of education, and became eager reformers themselves, both of Physical Education and school life in their home countries.

Following the English example, Baron Pierre de Coubertin and his friends were able to reform the French secondary schools before he applied the central educational principle of the Public Schools (that playing the game is more important than winning the match) to his Olympic principle: participating in the Olympic Games is more important to the youth of the world than winning a medal for a performance achieved.

Games and sports were introduced into French secondary schools with the educational objective to strive for best personal achievement and to compare achievement in competition with others. De Coubertin and his friends were not alone in their convictions. After 1880 more men, including Balck, Hertel, Schenckendorff, Kemeny, and Vikelas, considered individual and team competition in games and sport to be a valuable means of education, and reformed Physical Education in Sweden, Denmark, Germany, Austria-Hungary, and also in the mother country of the Olympic Games, Greece.

These sportsmen and early sponsors of the Olympic movement were concerned about the personal development of the achievement of youth in competitions against each other. The experience of one's effort, the sense of striving for individual improvement, and the personal experience of being part of a community with the same interests - these were the educational objectives which were held to be far more important than the results (best, second or third), scores or records achieved. In this respect losing, or not achieving the best score, i.e. the actual result, was of secondary importance. The athletic experience of achievement and performance in competition with others, i.e. the process, was the true objective.

Current Problems

This result may be surprising after one hundred years of the Olympic movement because a process of drastic change has taken place during this period; championships and records are today of utmost importance. This is exactly the underlying reason why increasingly more physical educators during the last twenty years neither use top level sport as an example for Physical Education in schools, nor recognise the objectives of the commercialised professional sports as an educational model.

Performance and achievement have been discredited as a traditional educational objective of Physical Education in schools. Some physical educators and scientific sports educators even believe that the motivation for achievement has lost its ideological veil and shows its true face today. They see inhuman top level sports with doping manipulations and winning at all costs - even at the cost of endangering one's health, and using all possible tricks to hurt the opponent. It is no wonder that a responsible educational objective is no longer visible for Physical Education in schools in this distorted dimension of top level sports, and the consequent inherent motivation for achievement.

The current problem is that through the progressive distorted development of top level sport, new characteristics of the spirit of achievement have appeared, which have consistently replaced and concealed the original process of character-building as an educational sense of achievement by a broadened conception of achievement as a product.

Along with the professionalism of top level sport, records have become a measure of athletic meetings. With the commercialism of top level sport, championships have become the objective of athletic meetings. Also together with the media involvement in top level sport, the athlete has become a vehicle for non-sport related results, whether as a representative of an image, or as a stamp of quality for a product either of an economic nature or as a service to a business. The human capital, the athlete as a transformer of non-sport-related results, now must advance professionalism and commercialism via records and championships. Both characteristics of the spirit of achievement form the conditions for a new role for the athlete: as representative of an image in the mass media. It is admittedly difficult for Physical Education teachers and scientific sport educators to recognise the present manifestation of top level sport, with its obvious emphasis on the modern 'product character', with its emphasis on achievement, as an educationally responsible, ethically moral example, and to accept the task of imparting this to children and youth.

For many educators, top level sport, and the Olympic spirit in particular, have revealed their true characters and have made a mess of themselves. And indeed, the philosophy of the Olympic Movement - formerly a stimulating spirit of achievement as a 'process' with an educational task - has vanished.

On one hand the spirit of achievement as an educational aim of Physical Education in schools has lost its credibility today, and teachers cannot recognise an educational value in making their students acquainted with top level sport. On the other hand, however, changes in society have taken place not only in top level sport, but also in schools and in learning methods during the last thirty years.

Parallel to the development of top level sport, the athletic value of popular sport has also been removed in many countries. New forms of sport with action and thrills, but also with risk and fun, have been developed with new, and especially individual, values of physical activity. They leave out the spirit of competition and performance very consciously, as is seen in the New Games Movement. Consequently, new attributes and standards for Physical Education in schools were incorporated in some countries during the 1980s and 1990s.
Seen from a historical point of view there are no objections to this development; after all Physical Education with its objectives and subjects

has always been a reflection of the times and of the era. The fact that makes the situation precarious is the following educational dilemma. On one hand, the spirit of achievement with its original educational tasks within Physical Education has been diminished with the progressive development of modern top level sport. It is threatened with being lost today due to new trends and expanded assignments within Physical Education. On the other hand, the new trends and objectives of Physical Education are not a substitute for the old spirit of achievement, nor do they adequately replace the lost educational aim of the original spirit of achievement.

Achievement and performance as educational aims of Physical Education cannot be discredited pedagogically by morally justified scruples against the manifestations of modern top level sport. There is an argument for replacing achievement as an aim of modern Physical Education with alternative moral concepts and other educational objectives. The result is, however, an educational vacuum.

Task for the Future

What are the perspectives for the future? What are the problems to be solved? The answer is easy: the clock cannot be turned back – nor is it desirable to seek to do this. The developed educational vacuum needs to be filled responsibly by a new pedagogical education of achievement.

As games and sport were introduced into Physical Education in schools in European countries they gradually became means to fulfil educational aims. Only when in the course of history games and sports became independent subjects in school did they lose their ties to educational objectives. These have been increasingly substituted by non-school related, and partially non-educational, objectives during the last thirty years.

Today's new trends in sport cannot serve as a principle of identification for moving into Physical Education without an educational objective. We can learn from Guthsmuths that physical activities other than those of the world of sport have to contribute to 'educational achievement' if they wish to be part of the school curriculum.

We need a new culture of achievement in Physical Education.

This new culture of achievement may neither be equated with the realisation of the collective industrial product 'top level sport', nor may it find its identity in the individual hedonism of living and trying post-modern 'movement practice'. Additionally, contradictory concepts must be resolved so that they do not become excessively ideological. Like athletic performance, development in Physical Education needs to qualify educationally, the new movement-orientated educational objectives of Physical Education need an achievement-orientated requirement for their optimal realisation.

'General sport' from 'outside' may focus as little attention on Physical Education in its educational perspective as 'individual education of Physical Education from 'inside' may exclude the subject of sport. On the one hand the object of modern sport imparted through Physical Education should avoid an educational shortage, on the other hand an educational limitation in the objectives of instruction should avoid a reduction to athletic experience.

Physical Education must be criticised ethically and morally when it does not consider the required performance of the students from an individual point of view, and fails to take into account pedagogical responsibility. In the same way, movement education can be criticised when it does not involve the complex world of sport by striving for educational objectives for students, while consciously excluding athletic achievements.

The task for the future is to bring the lost 'character process' of athletic achievement, as an educational aim of Physical Education, to the forefront again without focusing solely on traditional patterns of top level sport, or modern elements of recreational sport.

References

ADL (Hrsg.) (1962). Der Wetteifer. Frankfurt/Main: Limpert.

Andrieu, G. (1990). *L'education physique au XXe siècle. Une histoire des pratiques.* Joinville-le-Pont: Libraire du Sport.

Berg-Sørensen, I., Jørgensen, P. (Red.) (1998*). Een Time Dagligen, Skoleidræt gennem 200 år.* Odense: Universitetsforlag.

Brettschneider W.-D., Richartz, A. (1996*). Weltmeister werden und die Schule schaffen.* Schorndorf: Hofmann.

Bührle, M., Schnurr, M. (1991*). Leistungssport Herausforderung für die Sportwissenschaft. Kongreßbericht dvs 1989.* Schorndorf: Hofmann.

Clement, J.P., Herr, M. (eds.) (1993*). L'identité de l'éducation physique scolaire au XXe siècle.* Clermont-Ferrand: AFRAPS.

Coubertin, P. de (1936). *Olympische Erinnerungen.* Berlin: Limpert.

Digel, H. (1993).*Wettkampfsport – Wege zu einer besseren Praxis.* Aachen: Meyer & Meyer.

Dimitriou, M. (1995). *Leibeserziehung und Sport in Griechenland 1829-1914.* St. Augustin: Academia.

Fischer, R.J. & Borms, J. (1990). *The Search for Sporting Excellence.* Schorndorf: Hofmann.

Funke, J. (Hrsg.) (1983). *Sportunterricht als Körpererfahrung.* Reinbek: Rowohlt

Größing, S. (1993). *Bewegungskultur und Bewegungserziehung.* Schorndorf: Hofmann.

Grupe, O. (1982). *Bewegung, Spiel und Leistung im Sport.* Schorndorf: Hofmann.

Grupe, O. (1997). *Olympischer Sport*. Schorndorf: Hofmann.

Gutsmuths, J.C.F. (1793). *Gymnastik für die Jugend*. Schnepfenthal: Buchhandlung der Erziehungsanstalt.

Guttmann, A., (1979).Vom Ritual zum Rekord: *Das Wesen des modernen Sports*. Schorndorf: Hofmann.

Hamer, E.U. (1989). *Die Anfänge der "Spielbewegung" in Deutschland*. London: Arena.

Hardmann, K., Standeven, J. (eds.) (1998). *Cultural Diversity and Congruence in Physical Education and Sport*. Aachen: Meyer & Meyer.

Howald, H. , Hahn, E. (eds.) (1982). *Kinder im Leistungssport*. Basel: Birkhäuser.

John, H.G., Naul, R. (eds.) (1988). *Jugendsport im ersten Drittel des 20. Jahrhunderts*. Clausthal-Zellerfeld: Greinert.

Lindroth, J. (1993). Gymnastik med Lek och Idrott. *För och mot fria kroppsövningar i det svenska läroverket 1878-1928*. Stockholm: HLS Förlag.

MacAloon, J.J. (1981). *This great symbol: Pierre de Coubertin and the origins of the modern Olympic Games.* Chicago: University Press.

Mangan, J.A. (1981). *Athleticism in the Victorian and Edwardian public school.* Cambridge: University Press.

Meinander, H. (1994). *Towards a Bourgois Manhood – Boy's Physical Education in Nordic Secondary Schools 1880-1940*. Helsinki: The Finnish Society of Sciences and Letters.

Naul, R. (ed.) (1985). *Körperlichkeit und Schulturnen im Kaiserreich*. Wuppertal: Putty.

Naul, R., Hardman, K., Piéron, M., Skirstad, B., (eds.). (1998). *Physical Activity and Active Lifestyle of Childen and Youth*. Schorndorf: Hofmann .

Pawelke, R. (Hrsg.) (1995). *Neue Sportkultur*. Butzbach/Griedel: Afra-Verlag

Shields, D.L., Bredemeier B.J. (1995). *Character development and physical activity*. Champaign, IL.: Human Kinetics.

Siedentop, D. (1994). *Sport Education. Quality PE Through Positive Sport Experiences*. Champaign, IL.: Human Kinetics.

Treutlein, G., Funke. J., Sperle, N. (1992). *Körpererfahrung im Sport*. ADH-Schriftenreihe. Aachen: Meyer & Meyer.

Wopp, Ch.(1995). *Entwicklungen und Perspektiven des Freizeitsports*. Aachen: Meyer & Meyer.

SCHOOL SPORT AND COMPETITION: SPORTS PHYSIOLOGY

Neil Armstrong

Introduction

Young people are not mini-adults. They are growing and maturing at their own rate and their physiological responses to physical activity vary as they progress through childhood and adolescence into adult life. In this paper I will briefly review relevant aspects of growth and maturity (see Malina and Bouchard, 1991 for a detailed discussion) and examine their interaction with participation in youth sport.

Growth and Maturation

Growth and maturation are often used synonymously but they describe different processes. Growth refers to an increase in the size of the body or its parts whereas maturation refers to the tempo and timing of progress towards the mature or adult biological state.

Stature

Children tend to follow the same pattern of growth in stature and body mass, but there are major individual differences in both timing and magnitude of changes. Stature increases rapidly during the first 2 years of life and by the age of 2 the child has attained about 50% of adult stature.

Correspondence to: Professor Neil Armstrong, Children's Health and Exercise Research Centre, University of Exeter, St. Luke's Campus, Heavitree Road, Exeter, EX1 2LU, United Kingdom

The rate of increase in stature, however, falls continuously from birth onwards and reaches its lowest point just before the initiation of the pubertal growth spurt. The start of the pubertal growth spurt is subject to wide individual variations. It may begin as early as 7 ½ or as late as 10 years of age in girls, whereas in boys it normally occurs within the range 8 ½ to 12 ½ years of age. In girls, the growth spurt usually begins at about 9 years with the peak rate of growth in stature occurring just before 12 years of age, and adult stature being attained by 16 years. Boys lag about 2 years behind girls and generally attain adult stature by age 18. Although boys do experience a more pronounced pubertal growth spurt than girls the sex difference in adult stature, of about 13cm, is largely due to boys having the advantage of 2 years extra prepubertal growth.

Body Mass and Composition

The pattern of change in body mass during the pubertal growth spurt is similar to that of stature but it trails a few months behind. Girls gain about 33.5 kg between the ages of 7 and 18 years whereas boys experience a gain in mass of about 43.8 kg over the same period. The increase in boys' body mass is primarily due to increases in skeletal tissue and muscle mass with fat mass remaining stable. Girls experience less dramatic increases in muscle mass but a significant increase in fat mass over the same period.

Pre-pubertal girls have only slightly more body fat than boys but during the growth spurt girls' body fat increases to about 25% of body mass while boys decline to about 13% body fat. Muscle mass increases with age in both sexes and for a short period during early adolescence girls may have more muscle mass than boys. By the age of 13 girls' muscle mass may be 45% of body mass but, in relative terms, it declines thereafter due to increased fat accumulation. By the end of adolescence boys' muscle mass is about 54% of their body mass. These changes in body composition have significant effects on performance in activities where the strength: mass ratio is important.

Sexual Maturity

At puberty, both boys and girls undergo changes in their secondary sex characteristics but there is no consistent relationship between the age at which a child enters puberty and the rate of progression to maturity. Boys' testicles and penises enlarge and hair grows in the pubic region. The pubertal spurt in stature normally occurs after the beginning of testicular enlargement and the penis is growing maximally and pubic hair is usually well advanced before the most rapid growth in stature takes place. The breaking of the voice and the appearance of facial hair tend to occur relatively late in puberty. The advent of the breast bud is normally the first event to be noticed in girls, but it is not unusual for the appearance of pubic hair to occur before breast bud. Menarche, the age at which menstruation begins, occurs relatively late in puberty following the period of rapid growth in stature.

Muscle Strength

Boys' muscle strength increases linearly with age from early childhood until about 13 or 14 years of age when there is a marked increase in strength through the pubertal years, followed by a slower increase into the early or mid-twenties. Girls experience an almost linear increase in strength until about 15 years of age with no clear evidence of an adolescent spurt. Sex-related differences in strength have been reported in children as early as 3 years of age but the magnitude is small prior to puberty, and there is considerable overlap of male and female scores. The small pre-pubertal strength difference between boys and girls is markedly increased during adolescence, and few girls can match similarly aged boys on strength measures at this time. The sex-related difference is more marked in the arms and in the trunk than in the legs even after adjusting for differences in body size (Armstrong and Welsman, 1997).

During puberty marked differences in body shape become apparent between the sexes (and between early and late maturers of the same sex). Boys significantly increase their shoulder width in relation to the rest of their body whereas girls experience a similar spurt in hip width. Boys' greater shoulder width provides an anchorage for an increased upper trunk muscle mass and this contributes to the much greater sex-difference in upper body strength compared to leg strength. When this is coupled with boys' longer arms the reason why boys generally outperform girls in throwing and racquet sports becomes readily apparent.

Anaerobic and Aerobic Performance

All forms of exercise rely on muscle contraction and for this to occur energy is required. The muscles have three systems through which energy may be generated. Two of these systems do not require oxygen and are called anaerobic systems; the third system is dependent upon the delivery of oxygen to the muscles and is termed the aerobic system. During exercise no single energy system operates in isolation, but high intensity activity of short duration (e.g. sprinting) is primarily fuelled by the anaerobic systems whereas prolonged activity of moderate intensity (e.g. jogging) depends predominantly upon the aerobic system.

Boys' anaerobic performance increases with age from childhood through adolescence and into adult life. Recent evidence has demonstrated that there is a positive maturational effect on anaerobic performance independent of body size (Armstrong et al., 1997). Girls' anaerobic performance, however, appears to attain a minimal value during the teenage years and then stabilizes with a few minor variations. Sex-related differences in anaerobic performance are minimal during the prepubertal period, but during adolescence boys become significantly better anaerobic performers than girls, and they retain this advantage into adult life (Armstrong and Welsman, 1997)

Aerobic exercise is dependent upon the respiratory and cardiovascular systems delivering oxygen to the muscles and the ability of the exercising muscles to use the oxygen delivered. As maximal aerobic exercise is limited by peak oxygen uptake (peak VO_2) this variable is widely recognized as the best single index of children's and adolescents aerobic fitness. Boys' peak VO_2 increases by about 150% over the age range 8 to 16 years, whereas girls demonstrate an 80% increase over the same time period. At age 10 boys' peak VO_2 is about 12% higher than that of girls, and by age 16 the difference between the sexes increases to about 37% in favour of boys. The sex difference between adolescents' peak VO_2 values has been attributed to boys greater muscle mass and haemoglobin concentration (Armstrong and Welsman, 1994)

As most physical activity involves moving body mass from one place to another, peak VO_2 is usually expressed in relation to body mass. With this convention a different picture emerges from that apparent when absolute values are used. Boys' mass-related peak VO_2 is remarkably stable over the age range 8 to 16 years, implying that their aerobic fitness increases in direct proportion with body mass. Girls demonstrate a decrease in mass-related peak VO_2 with age which is related to the accumulation of body fat during adolescence. Boys' mass-related peak VO_2 values are significantly higher than those of girls, at least from the age of 10 years (Armstrong and Welsman, 1997). Although conventional analysis suggests that there is no maturational effect on aerobic fitness, above that due to body size recent work has demonstrated that when body size is appropriately controlled, using allometric techniques, there is a positive maturational effect on aerobic fitness independent of body size in both boys and girls (Armstrong et al., 1998).

GROWTH, MATURATION AND COMPETITIVE SPORT

Growth and Maturation of Young Adults

Successful adult athletes tend to have body structures that favour their specific sport with tallness being a characteristic of athletes in many sports. Similarly, participants in youth sport have, on average, statures that equal or exceed the reference median, although there are exceptions such as gymnasts, where short stature is common in both sexes (Malina, 1994). Does exercise training for competitive sport therefore influence body size and composition?

Stature

Young athletes are a special population who are selected not only for specific skills but also according to characteristics of body size. It is very difficult to assess exercise training effects on body size when youngsters may be shorter than average (e.g. gymnasts), or taller than average (e.g. swimmers) prior to the start of their respective training programmes. For example, parents of swimmers are generally taller than those of gymnasts, implying a genotypic factor in stature (Malina, 1994). Boys who are successful in many sports during childhood, and especially in early adolescence, tend to be more advanced in biological maturity status, and hence taller than their similarly aged peers. Data on young athletes therefore need to be considered in the context of initial selection, and when this is taken into account both longitudinal and cross-sectional studies indicate that the stature attained by participants in competitive youth sport does not appear to be affected by intensive training.

Body Mass and Composition

Body mass and composition can be influenced by exercise training. Decreases in body fatness are associated with training in both sexes, and this effect may be augmented by dietary restrictions in young sportspersons (e.g. gymnastics in girls and wrestling in boys) (Malina, 1994). Increases in muscle mass with resistance training in adolescent boys are well-documented, but there is little evidence of resistance training-induced muscle hypertrophy in girls and prepubertal boys even in studies that report significant increases in muscle strength (Blimkie and Sale, 1998). Cross-sectional studies have generally indicated a positive effect of resistance training and body mass supporting exercise on bone mineral density (BMD) (Bailey and Martin, 1994) but, the only well-controlled prospective study of young people to date reported no significant changes in whole body BMD, or lumbar spine BMD following 6 months of resistance training (Blinkie et al., 1993).

Sexual Maturation

Girls who are successful in youth sports tend to be delayed in menarche and the possibility that exercise training may delay sexual maturation has been comprehensively debated (Malina, 1994). In contrast, successful young male athletes tend to be advanced in maturation. The explanation may lie in preselection for certain sports. Boys participate more in team games and sports which depend upon strength and power; the boy with advanced pubertal development is therefore at a distinct advantage. Conversely, the characteristics associated with delayed maturation in females may be more suitable for performance in activities popular with girls, such as gymnastics and dance. Late maturing girls tend to be more linear in shape, longer-legged, narrower-hipped, and less fat than their maturing peers (Armstrong and Welsman, 1997).

The literature describing menarcheal age in selected groups of female athletes is extensive, but although it is often inferred that training "delays" menarche it has yet to be shown that there is a causal relationship. Menarche is influenced by a number of social and biocultural variables and, in adequately nourished individuals, sexual maturation is a genotypically mediated process. If exercise training and participation in competitive sport are associated with later menarche the relationship is confounded by other interacting factors so that the specific effects of exercise are difficult to assess (Malina, 1994)

Young people with an adequate diet will grow and mature regardless of their participation in competitive sport. There is no compelling evidence that exercise training and competition affects stature, rate of growth or indices of sexual maturation.

Muscle Strength

Adolescents respond to resistance training programmes with significant increases in muscle strength, although girls may experience a less dramatic response to that seen in boys. There is a popular view that resistance training programmes are ineffective with prepubescent children. This is not based on sound scientific evidence, and well-controlled studies have clearly demonstrated that appropriate resistance training programmes can induce increases in muscle strength during childhood. Prepubescent children do not normally experience significant increases in muscle size with resistance training, and it appears that observed increases in strength are primarily due to neurological adaptation. Significant increases in muscle fibre recruitment (motor unit activation) have been noted following resistance training and this, coupled with improvements in motor co-ordination, is the likely explanation for prepubescent strength increases in the absence of muscle hypertrophy (Blinkie and Sale, 1998).

Unfortunately, training-induced strength gains will not persist through a period of detraining, and once training ceases its effects begin to decay.

The long-term benefits of resistance training depend upon the maintenance of the programme into adult life.

Anaerobic and Aerobic Performance

The effects of exercise training on children's and adolescents' anaerobic performance are not well-documented. This is somewhat surprising as many of young people's activities, both recreational and in competitive sport, involve brief bursts of activity performed at high intensity. Studies that have examined anaerobic performance in young people, before and after a period of exercise training, have noted improvements in biochemical markers of anaerobic energy provision and anaerobic performance, but data are inconsistent and confounded by ethical and methodological problems associated with the assessment of anaerobic performance. The weight of evidence suggests that although appropriate exercise training will induce increases in young people's anaerobic performance the magnitude of change is generally less than that observed in adults (Armstrong and Welsman, 1997).

Exercise training programmes of the appropriate frequency, intensity, duration and mode of exercise will induce, in both boys and girls, increases in peak VO_2. Other beneficial adaptations to the cardiopulmonary system which have been reported include increases in heart volume, blood volume, total haemoglobin, maximal stroke volume, maximal tidal volume and maximal pulmonary ventilation. As with anaerobic performance the size of the changes may be less than those expected with adult subjects. It has been suggested that there is a critical time period in a child's life (a "trigger point") below which the effects of training will be minimal, or will not occur at all (Katch, 1983). The evidence is, however, equivocal, and the case for a maturational threshold of enhanced aerobic responses to exercise training remains to be proven (Armstrong and Welsman, 1997).

Training during childhood and adolescence does not induce permanent increases in anaerobic and aerobic fitness, and it appears that the long-term benefits of exercise on both anaerobic and aerobic energy systems depend upon the continuance of appropriate exercise training into adult life.

Seasonal Birth Distribution

Youth competition is inevitably based on chronological age and this gives the individual born in the early part of the selection year a marked advantage over those born later in the year. The phenomenon has been documented in soccer players, tennis players and hockey players (Baxter-Jones, 1995) with perhaps the most striking example being Brewer et al's (1995) analysis of the birth dates of players selected for the Football Association's School of Excellence. About 16 14 year old boys are selected annually, and the birth distribution of the 103 boys selected over a 6 year period showed that 67% were born in the first 3 months of the selection year and less than 2% in the last 3 months. Eighty nine percent of the boys were born in the first half of the selection year.

This unequal distribution of the birth dates persists into the senior game where almost half of the English senior professional players were born in the first third of the selection year. Even at the highest level 48% of the players to represent England in the World Cup tournaments from 1986 to 1998 were born in the first third of the selection year compared with 23% in the final third. The residual bias as a result of selection policies at junior level may be because these players are exposed to high levels of coaching at an early age and become known to selectors. Many talented youngsters are overlooked because they were unfortunate enough to be born at the wrong time.

Overuse Injuries

Intensive training and competition may start at a young age, and young people involved in this type of exercise are at risk of two major categories of musculoskeletal injury. The first of these, injury due to a single acute "macrotrauma", is a risk of sports regardless of age and is the predominant source of athletic injury. Acute fractures are typical of this type of injury but, in children, additional bony injuries are often observed. These include plastic deformation, torus fracture, greenstick fractures, acute epiphyseal plate injury and acute apophyseal avulsion (Maffuli, 1995).

The sequel of unresolved, repeated "microtrauma" comprise the second type of injury characteristic of intensive exercise at a young age. Stress fractures typically result from inappropriate training programmes. The points at which the major tendons attach to bone are particular areas at risk of overuse injury in the young athlete. Overstress to these points can disrupt the process of ossification leading to chronic inflammation, avulsion of cartilage and bone from the developing area with tendinous microtears and haemorrhages. The damage and fragmentation to bone is called osteochondritis. Repetitive jarring of the joints leads to osteochondritis dessicans which is a disorder of the joint surfaces which occurs when segments of subchondral bone and articular cartilage become avascular, die and separate from the underlying bone forming a loose body (see Maffuli, 1995 for further details of overuse injuries in young people).

Overuse injuries are provoked by a variety of factors including incorrect and overzealous training, the "too much too soon" phenomenon, poor techniques in throwing or contact sports, poorly fitting footwear or protective gear, and excess pressure from parents and/or coaches. Overuse injuries can be prevented by ensuring that training programmes, and frequency and type of competition, are appropriately geared to the young athlete's maturity stage, combined with sufficient rest to allow restitution of any microtrauma. Should injury occur correct and complete rehabilitation is essential before return to full training and competition given the serious long-term consequences if overuse injuries are prolonged.

School Sport, Competition and Physical Education

Young people grow and mature at their own pace, and as they progress through early childhood and adolescence into young adulthood it is essential that they develop and refine the motor skills necessary to successfully and enjoyably participate in various forms of physical activity. In relation to their growth and maturation children and adolescents need to be exposed to a balanced programme of competitive, co-operative, individual, partner and team activities to lay the foundation for present and future physical activity behaviour (Armstrong and Welsman, 1997).

Competitive sport is an essential component of young people's physical education. Many youngsters enjoy competitive sport and natural talent must be nurtured so that the gifted few fulfil their potential. But, too many young people are discouraged from participating in physical activity through lack of success in competitive sport. This may simply be because their individual biological clock is not running in accord with the calendar, or their birthday falls at the wrong time of the year. As many of the health benefits of physical activity manifest themselves in adult life, those involved in organising and coaching competitive school sport must focus on the importance of growth and maturation and its interaction with performance, and address the issues of promoting physical activities which are likely to be sustained into adult life. The role of school sport and competition is to promote the well-being of the child, it is not the role of the child to promote the well-being of competitive school sport.

References

Armstrong, N. & Welsman, J.R. (1994). Assessment and interpretation ofaerobic fitness in children and adolescents. *Exercise and Sport Sciences Reviews*, **22**, 435-76.

Armstrong, N. and Welsman, J.R. (1997). *Young People and Physical Activity*. Oxford: Oxford University Press.

Armstrong, N., Welsman, J.R. and Kirby, B.J. (1997). Performance on the Wingate Anaerobic Test and Maturation. *Pediatric Exercise Science*, **9**, 253-61.

Armstrong, N., Welsman, J.R. and Kirby, B.J. (1998). Peak oxygen uptake and maturation in 12-yr olds. *Medicine and Science in Sports and Exercise*, **30**,165-169.

Bailey, D.A. and Martin, A.D. (1994). Physical activity and skeletal health in adolescents. *Pediatric Exercise Science,* **6**, 330-47.

Baxter-Jones, A.D.G. (1995). *Growth and development of young athletes. Sports Medicine*, **20**, 59-64.

Blimkie, C.J.R., Rice, S., Webber, C., Martin, J., Levy, D. and Gordon, C. (1993). Effects of resistance training on bone mass and density in adolescent females. *Medicine and Science in Sports and Exercise*, **25**, S48.

Blimkie, C.J.R. and Sale, D.G. (1998). Strength development and trainability during childhood. In E. Van Praagh (Ed.), *Pediatric Anaerobic Performance*. Champaign, Illinois, Human Kinetics, pp. 193-224.

Brewer, J., Balsom, P. and Davis, J. (1995). Seasonal birth distribution amongst European soccer players. *Sports Exercise and Injury*, **1**, 154-7.

Katch, V.L. (1983). Physical conditioning of children. *Journal of Adolescent Health Care*, **3**, 241-6.

Maffuli, N., Ed. (1995). *Color Atlas and Text of Sports Medicine in Childhood and Adolescence.* London, Mosby-Wolfe.

Malina, R.M. (1994). Physical growth and biological maturation of young athletes. *Exercise and Sport Sciences Reviews*, **22**, 389-433.

Malina, R.M. and Bouchard, C. (1991). *Growth, Maturation and Physical Activity.* Champaign, Illinois, Human Kinetics.

Non-Specialist Bibliography

Grisogono, V. (1991). *Children and Sport: Fitness Injuries and Diet.* London, Murray.

Lee, M., Ed. (1993). *Coaching Children in Sport.* London, E and FN Spon.

Malina, R.M. and Bouchard, C. (1991). *Growth, Maturation and Physical Activity.* Champaign, Illinois, Human Kinetics.

Rowland, T.W. (1990). *Exercise and Children's Health.* Champaign, Illinois, Human Kinetics; pages 74-76.

Smoll, F.L. and Smith, R.E., Eds. (1996). *Children and Youth in Sport.* Madison, IA, Brown and Benchmark.

Specialist Bibliography

Armstrong, N. and Van Mechelen, W., Eds. (1999). *Textbook of Paediatric Exercise Science and Medicine.* Oxford, Oxford University Press.

Armstrong, N. and Welsman, J.R. (1994). Assessment and interpretation of aerobic fitness in children and adolescents. *Exercise and Sport Sciences Reviews*, **22**, 435-76.

Armstrong, N. and Welsman, J.R. (1997). *Young People and Physical Activity.* Oxford, Oxford University Press.

Bar-Or, O., Ed. (1996). *The Child and Adolescent Athlete*. Oxford, Blackwell.

Cahill, B.R. and Pearl, A.J., Eds. (1993*). Intensive Participation in Children's Sports*. Champaign, Illinois, Human Kinetics.

Chan, K.-M. and Micheli, L.J., Eds. (1998). *Sports and Children*. Hong Kong, Williams and Wilkins.

Maffuli, N., Ed. (1995). *Color Atlas and Text of Sports Medicine in Childhood and Adolescence*. London, Mosby-Wolfe.

Malina, R.M. (1994). Physical growth and biological maturation of young athletes. *Exercise and Sport Sciences Reviews*, **22**, 389-433.

Rowland, T.W. (1996). *Developmental Exercise Physiology*. Champaign, Illinois, Human Kinetics.

Van Praagh, E. (1998). *Pediatric Anaerobic Performance*. Champaign, Illinois, Human Kinetics.

Perspectives, 1999, Vol. 1: 99-113
School Sport and Competition

SCHOOL SPORT AND COMPETITION: SPORTS PSYCHOLOGY

Toward an Integrated Sport Science Approach to Youth Sport Research and Practice

Maureen R. Weiss

Introduction

The millions of youth participating in organized sport programs around the world reflect the important role that the physical domain plays in children's lives. While most children and adolescents tell us that improving skills, making friends, and having fun are the most salient reasons for participating in sport, researchers, educators and parents understand the more far-reaching consequences of participating in daily physical activity. It has long been recognized that sport participation has the potential for contributing substantively to the physical, psychological, and social development of youngsters. Moreover, vigorous activity in most sports and games can also provide the adequate cardiovascular and musculoskeletal requirements for maintaining a healthy lifestyle, and contribute to a positive attitude about the value of physical activity across the lifespan. It is for these reasons that the topic of youth sports is and will remain a central interest for sport science researchers and practitioners.

Over the last decade, research on children and adolescents in sport has flourished. This interest is characterized by the number of books, and academic and anecdotal articles on various aspects of youth sports. This

Correspondence to: Dr. Maureen R. Weiss, Professor, Sport and Exercise Psychology, Health and Physical Education, 201 Memorial Gymnasium, Curry School of Education, University of Virginia, Charlottesville, VA 22903 USA.

research and its implications for practitioners have traditionally been quite specialized in nature, with a focus on either the biological, social, psychological, or physical characteristics associated with active participation in sport. This paper will advocate an integration of the sub-disciplines within the sport science as a necessary direction for youth sport research in order to best understand the underlying processes and consequences of activity involvement. An integrated sport science approach is one that combines scientific knowledge from such areas as sport psychology, motor learning and control, exercise physiology, and biomechanics, to describe, explain, and predict participation behavior and performance in sport settings. Moreover, such an approach will help explain more of the variables that contribute to participation behaviors, as well as respond to the need for providing practitioners with information they can use to understand and solve sport-specific problems.

Three purposes of the World Congress on Youth, Leisure, and Physical Activity, held in Brussels, Belgium in 1990, were outlined. These were: (a) exchange information about current research in youth sport, and directions for future research and theory developments; (b) bring field workers and policy makers into contact with research findings (and I would add bringing researchers into contact with experimental findings), (c) foster communication among the many areas of research in youth, leisure, and sport, because the field is fragmented. These three purposes necessarily bring into light two important issues. First, the most current research within and across the sport science disciplines must be shared and discussed. Because physical, biological, social, and psychological factors impact upon a child's development through sport, we can no longer continue to view the child as a fragmented being, but one who is continually influenced by a number of interacting variables. Second, researchers and practitioners must face important issues concerning youth sports hand-in-hand. This translates to more open communication and willingness to co-operate on issues that will positively influence children and youth in sport. For example, researchers can make more of an effort to ask research questions that practitioners consider to be salient, while practitioners can make an effort to implement recommendations made by researchers for modifying children's sport in order to achieve physical and psychosocial development goals.

In light of these issues, the remainder of the paper will center around three major themes. First, the current status of youth sport psychological research will be reviewed. Trends with regard to the current status and quantity of research, theoretical orientations, and most frequent research topics will be the focus. Second, an integrated sport science approach will be advocated through the introduction of biological, physical, psychological, and social factors. Finally, directions for encouraging more research in youth sports from an integrated perspective will be provided. It is hoped that the approach of this paper will result in an awareness of the need to consider the 'whole child' as well as the numerous contributing influences impacting upon children's participation in sport.

Current Status of Youth Sport Research

Over the last decade there has been an explosion of research studies in the area of youth sports. This knowledge can be categorized under four areas: (a) biological, such as information provided by exercise physiology and growth and development research; (b) psychological, provided by researchers in sport psychology and motor learning and control; (c) social, characterized by findings by both sport sociologists and psychologists; (d) physical, such as information revealed by biomechanics and motor development research. Moreover, this information base, for the most part, has been very specialized without considering the contribution of influences from the other areas of development. To illustrate this point, past and recent developments of the psychological development of youth in sport can be examined. Systematic, empirical research on the psychological aspects of youth sport involvement has evolved most over the last 15 years. Early research primarily addressed questions such as characteristics and attitudes of youth sport coaches (Gould & Martens, 1978; Weiss & Gould, 1979), whether youth sport competition is too stressful (Scanlan & Passer, 1978, 1979; Simon & Martens, 1979), and the relationship between coaching behaviors and motivational consequences for participation (Smith, Smoll & Curtis, 1979; Smith, Smoll & Hunt, 1977; Smoll, Smith, Curtis & Hunt, 1978). In a major review paper, Gould (1982) outlined the status and future directions of youth sport research in the 1980's. He believed that key research studies in the area of sport psychology were characterized by testing or developing psychological theory, and asking questions of practical significance. He advocated that future research should follow this lead as well as incorporate a variety of methodological approaches such as the use of multivariate designs, more longitudinal research, multiple assessment techniques, and team research of a multidisciplinary nature.

Weiss and Bredemeier (1983) encouraged a complementary but different approach to that of Gould (1982). They advocated a cognitive developmental theoretical orientation to the study of children's psychological development through sport. A cognitive developmental perspective is focused upon those ontogenetic changes in cognitive abilities that help to describe and explain psychosocial and behavioral variations among individuals differentiated by developmental levels. Examples of such an approach include Piaget's stages of cognitive development and Kohlberg's stages of moral reasoning. The authors argued that such an approach must necessarily take into account cognitive and/or biological maturation in order to understand behavioral changes in children and youth. In a content analysis of major academic journals and books spanning the years 1970-1982, 143 studies and reviews were identified that focused exclusively on the psychological aspects of youth sport. However, only about 10% (n = 15) of these papers employed a cognitive developmental theoretical perspective by either selection of age groups based on a underlying cognitive criteria, or utilizing information from the developmental psychology literature to offer implications for understanding children's development through sport.

A follow-up content analysis was recently carried out to the one conducted in the Weiss and Bredemeier (1983) paper. Journal articles and book chapters on psychological aspects of youth sport involvement which spanned the years from 1983 to 1990 were analyzed for cognitive development content, the testing or development of theory, and most popular areas of study. This analysis produced 163 studies and reviews; however, as in 1983, very few considered developmental or cognitive-developmental factors in their content. Despite this discouraging news, many studies were based on resting existing psychological theory (e.g. Harter's competence motivation theory. Weiner's attributional theory of achievement motivation, Bandura's self-efficacy theory), or attempted to develop sport-specific theories (e.g. Fox & Corbin, 1989; Scanlan & Simons, in press). Secondly, while Gould (1982) could only identify the research by Scanlan and Passer, and Smith and Smoll as major lines of research in youth sport, many additional research programs could be identified (e.g., Bredemeier at UC Berkeley: moral development; Weiss at University of Oregon: perceived competence; modeling; Horn at Miami University, Ohio: sources of physical competence information). Finally, the most frequent topics of research inquiry included: why children participate in and drop out from sport, stress and anxiety, and the development of perceived competence and its relationship to achievement characteristics.

Based on this content analysis, it was determined that contemporary youth sport research had followed Gould's (1982) recommendations of conducting research that tests or develops theory, as well as asking important questions that also have practical significance. However, contrary to his recommendations of methodology, incorporating multiple assessment techniques and team research of a multi-disciplinary nature, few studies characterized these attributes. Finally, the vast majority of this research has been conducted on white, middle or middle-upper class, well educated youth. Few studies of racial, ethnic, or cultural diversity could be found. Thus, the results from this vast knowledge base may not generalize to other populations.

Toward an Integrated Sport Science Approach

Based on the current status of sport psychology research on youth, it is reasonable to believe that pediatric science research in the areas of motor learning and control, biomechanics, and exercise physiology is similar. That is, the research in these areas also primarily endorses a uni- rather than multi-disciplinary approach to answering questions, uses a limited number of assessment techniques, and derives its subject pools from the white, middle-class group. The purpose of this section is to not only advocate for an integrated sport science approach to the study of youth in sport, but also to provide a rationale for the approach and strategies for bringing about more research of this type. That is, many people talk about an integrated or multi-disciplinary approach to youth sport research but few are actually doing it. We must begin to identify research questions conductive to such an approach.

The rationale for implementing an integrated sport science approach to studying children in sport is fairly straightforward. The actual implementation, on the other hand, is a different story. Two major reasons underlie the pressing need for more inter-disciplinary research on youth. First, there is a need to identify more variables that influence participation and performance in applied sport settings. The use of psychological, physiological or physical characteristics alone is insufficient for under-standing participation patterns, short- and long-term performance, and the general health and well being of youngsters. Second, it is important that researchers respond to the need for providing practitioners to address issues such as attrition from sport, game modifications, and parental influences in youth sport. The spectrum of sociological, psychological, physical, and biological factors that influence these phenomena must be considered. In order to understand their influence, more integrated sport science research is necessary.

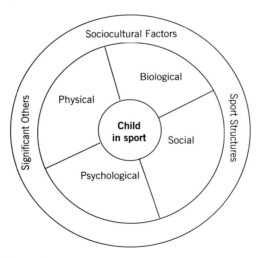

Figure 1. Child in sport

In order to depict the interactional nature of these characteristics on the young athlete, the 'wheel of child development' is meant to represent a model or schematic around which an integrated sport science approach can be organized (see Figure 1). There are three distinct qualities about the wheel of child development that *warrant* attention. First, the child in sport is influenced and characterized by a number of individual difference factors, represented by the closest outer circle to the child. These individual difference include physical e.g., body size, strength; biological e.g., maturity status, aerobic power; psychological e.g., self-esteem, motivation; and social e.g., peer acceptance, moral reasoning, develop-mental areas. These individual attributes distinguish children in sport and contribute to coloring their experiences as being positive or negative. Second the child is influenced by a number of social contextual factors, represented by the far outer circle of the diagram. These factors include significant others e.g., parents, peers; sociocultural attributes e.g., race, ethnicity; and the sport structure e.g., top level sport, leisure sport. Thus the child's experiences in sport are not only influenced by biological and psychological attributes per se, but also the social context in which these experiences occur.

Finally, the 'wheel' represents an open system, depicted by the open boundaries, whereby continuous reciprocal interactions can occur between the child, individual areas of development, and the social context. More specifically, individual difference factors can interact to influence the child's experiences, individual differences and social contextual factors, and finally the child can influence the system as well as being the object of influence. For example, the child's willingness to adhere to a training program is likely to have strong effects on his or her physical skills, physiological capacities, and psychological well being, as well as on the structure of family activities. As a result of the young athlete's increased commitment to the sport, and rise through the hierarchy of the sport structure, parents and siblings may have to work their schedules around the athlete's competitive commitments, and practice times, and perhaps sacrifice their own leisure time and money to invest in the child's athletic involvement. This child development wheel will be used further as an organizing theme for the notion of integrating sport science research.

A number of scholars in the areas of motor control, sport psychology, and motor development have been strongly advocating the integration of subdisciplines within the sport and exercise sciences (Christina, 1984, 1987; Feltz, 197; Malina, 1988; Roberton, 1988). They contend that both theoretical and applied research must come from an interdisciplinary knowledge base, such as considering the interaction between the human organism itself and social or environmental factors in order to best understand participation patterns and performance in the sport setting. Christina (1984), for example, suggests that artificial boundaries exist across subdisciplines and these need to be wiped out in areas where integration is necessary (represented by the open boundaries in the wheel). He suggests that one area that is a prime target for integrated research is youth sport. Christina (1984) states that youth sport has the potential to be a thread of similarity with which we can build connections between all of our subdisciplines in sport and exercise science.

If scholars across several areas are strongly advocating integrated sport science research, and the wheel of child development logically depicts the continuously interacting influences of individual differences and social contextual factors, one must ask the question, 'why has there been so little integrated research'? Three major reasons appear to exist for the death of interdisciplinary research in the area of youth sports. First, sport science researchers often have misperceptions, and sometimes suspicions, about each other's research areas. That is, because we tend to be very specialized we often do not understand what others are doing, including specific experimental designs, methodologies, and topics of inquiry. This lack of understanding may create stereotypes in people's minds about what characterizes the focus of research in such areas as biomechanics, sport psychology, exercise physiology, and motor control. For example, some individuals may perceive that sport psychology researchers only study methods such as mental imagery and stress management, without concern for the athlete's level of sport skill acquisition. Similarly, because motor control researchers tend to conduct highly controlled experimental studies using novel tasks, individuals may perceive these studies to be trivial, and lacking application. The point is that misperceptions about each other's research may often prevent us from conducting interdisciplinary studies. Open lines of communication and mutual respect are viable alternatives to mistrust and suspicion about other's research.

A second reason for the lack of interdisciplinary research is the extent of the knowledge base in each particular research area. As indicated earlier using sport psychology as an example, the number of studies and review papers is quite extensive in each of the areas of development. Because it is often difficult enough to stay contemporary in one's own area, let alone another sport science area, it is perhaps not surprising that integrated research studies are not more popular. Finally, different research designs and methodological approaches necessarily prevent more integration among the sub-disciplines. Some areas primarily depend upon basic research, in which controlled laboratory studies are conducted using experimental designs, without any requirement for making practical applications e.g., motor control, exercise physiology. Other areas adopt more applied research foci, consisting of correlational designs that are conducted in the "lab" or field using naturalistic tasks, with an interest in developing theory as well as making practical applications e.g., sport psychology, motor learning. Often the mixing of these designs, and/or methodologies, does not make interdisciplinary research conductive.

Recently Christina (1987) suggested that interdisciplinary research is most likely to occur when researchers ask questions that are theoretical as well as applied in nature, and are willing to commit a portion of their research study to multiple methods of investigation. That is, if sport psychology and motor control researchers collaborate, it will be necessary to conduct research at what Christina (1987) calls Level 2 Applied Research: testing hypotheses in a field, or lab setting, using sport skills where the goal is to develop theory-based knowledge for understanding the learning and performance of sport skills in naturalistic settings, with no requirement to find immediate solutions to sport-specific problems. For example, motor control research is often characterized by controlled laboratory research with a small sample size, a within-subject research design, numerous trials, and multiple dependent variables. Sport psychology research is also multivariate in nature, but with large samples, fewer trials, and between-subject research designs. In order to make inter-disciplinary research a reality between these areas, a particular sub-sample could be targeted for integrated and collaborative investigation.

So far in this paper I have described what integrated research can entail and why it is necessary for advancing the scientific and practical knowledge about youth sport phenomena. More specifically, integrated research is represented by the interweaving of ideas, theories, and methodologies among specific sport science areas. It is also characterized by the interaction between individual difference factors and social contextual factors. The wheel of child development schematic illuminates this notion of integrated research. The 'why' of integrated research focused on two major reasons: to identify more variables which contribute to participation and performance in sport settings, and to respond to the need for informing practitioners about how to solve sport-specific problems. The purpose of this last section of the manuscript is to address how integrated sport science research is most likely to occur, and examples of research that are conductive to an integrated, collaborative approach.

Steps toward bridging the gap that has prevented integrated research from occurring correspond directly with the major reasons contributing to this barrier. Specifically, these were misperceptions about each other's research, the extent of the knowledge base in each area, and differing methodologies used to answer research questions. One way of bridging the integration gap is to develop a mutual respect for each other's research through direct communication. To do so we must come out of our own "labs", discuss common research questions and interests, and how we can seek answers to these questions. We can also read each other's research in inter-disciplinary journals and books such as *Pediatric Exercise Science,* and *Advances in Pediatric Sports Sciences* (both published by Human Kinetics, USA). Perhaps more practically, we can directly communicate at conferences such that specifically focus on children in sport.

A second strategy for encouraging more integrated sport science research is to engage in collaborative research efforts. This would take care of the knowledge base problem, in that experts in each of the research areas can equally contribute to development of research questions, methodologies used, and roles and responsibilities. Collaborative research would also facilitate the use of multiple research methods, such as use of specific pieces of equipment, administration of self-report measures, and the conducting of in-depth interviews. Third, more integrated research can be encouraged by asking questions that test and develop theory in either "lab" or field settings with naturalistic tasks or skills – what Christina (1987) has labelled Level 2 Research. Finally specific research questions and goals that provide opportunities for integrated research must be identified. Not all questions are conductive to integration – thus the phrase 'integration but not obliteration' (Roberton, 1988). We must continue to contribute to our own specialized knowledge base, but be on the lookout for overlapping questions of interest. The research question is the key in determining whether integrated research is appropriate.

Several research questions pertaining to phenomena in youth sport appear to be pertinent and salient for collaborative inquiry among sport scientists. For example, the topic of readiness for sport competition necessarily entails an analysis of biological, physical and psychological attributes necessary for successful participation in sport. Malina very nicely outlines the major issues involved with the topic of readiness. Game modifications, and their influence on skill performance and perceived competence, join together issues related to biomechanics, motor learning, and sport psychology. Specifically, do adaptations made to adult-style games result in more technically correct skill execution, faster learning, less anxiety, and higher self-esteem? The topic of stress and anxiety is a natural one for collaborative efforts among pediatric sport psychologists and physiologists. The concern over injuries incurred as a result of athletic participation would bring together sports medicine and sport psychology researchers, with emphasis on physical and psychological factors related to rehabilitation from injury. Several other topics form a strong base for encouraging integrated sport science research on youth in sport.

Conclusion

This paper emphasized the need to adopt an integrated sport science approach to youth sport research and practice. The wheel of child development represents an organizing model for such an approach and visually displays the important interaction among the child, individual difference factors in development, and social contextual factors. One way of spinning the wheel into motion is to observe for ‚threads of similarity‘ between one's area of expertise and other areas that focus on pediatric exercise topics. Even though we should continue to enhance the knowledge base in our own specific areas of sport science, we must be on the lookout for connections to be made willing collaborators. Once we make the connection, we need to utilize multiple sources of knowledge to guide the research, including both scientific knowledge as well as experimental knowledge contributed by practitioners in the youth sport setting. Moreover, we must start interweaving the biological, psychological, social, and physical areas of development within the larger social context in which they occur. If we are able to accomplish these two objectives, theory to practice and integration of areas, then we will not only enhance the knowledge base of youth sport research, but enrich our own communication as scientists and practitioners as well.

References

Christina, R.W. (1984, May). *On the integration of scientific knowledge in sports psychology, motor development, and motor learning/control.* Paper presented at the R. Tait McKenzie Symposium on Sport. Knoxville, Texas.

Christina, R.W. (1987). Motor learning: Future lines of research'. In M.J. Sfrit & H.M. Eckert, eds. *The cutting edge in physical education and exercise science research. American Academy of Physical Education Papers*, nr. 20. Champaign, Illinois: Human Kinetics.

Feltz, D.L. (1987). The future of graduate education in sport and exercise science: A sport psychology perspective. *Quest*, **39**, pp. 2434-254.

Fox, K.R. & Corbin, C.B. (1989). The physical self-perception profile: Development and preliminary validation. *Journal of Sport Psychology*, **4**, pp. 203-218.

Gould, D. (1982). Sport for psychology in the 1980's: Status, direction, and challenge in youth sports research. *Journal of Sport Psychology*, **4**, pp. 203-218.

Gould, D. & Martens, R. (1979). Attitudes of volunteer coaches toward significant youth sport issues. *Research Quarterly*, 50, pp. 369-380.

Malina, R.M. (1988). Growth and maturation of young athletes: Biological and social considerations', in F. Smoll, R. Magill & M. Ash (Eds.) *Children in sport* (pp. 83-102). Champaign, Illinois: Human Kinetics.

Roberton, M.A: (1988): The weavers' loom: A developmental metaphor', in J. Clark & J. Humphrey (Eds.) *Advances in motor development research*, vol. 2. New York: AMS Press.

Scanlan, T.K. & Passer, M.W. (1978). Factors related to competitive stress among male youth sports participants. *Medicine and Science in Sport*, **10**, pp. 103-198.

Scanlan, T.K. & Passer, M.W. (1979). Sources of competitive stress in young female athletes. *Journal of Sport Psychology*, **1**, pp. 151-159.

Scanlan, T.K. & Simons, J.P. (1992). The construct of enjoyment. In G.C. Roberts (Ed.), *Motivation in sport and exercise.* Champaign, Illinois: Human Kinetics.

Simon, J.A. & Martens, R. Children's anxiety in sport and non-sport evaluative activities. *Journal of Sport Psychology*, **1**, pp. 160-169.

Smith, R.E. Smoll, F.L. & Curtis, B. (1979). Coach effectiveness training: A cognitive behavioral approach to enhancing relationship skills in youth sport coaches. *Journal of Sport Psychology*, **1**, pp. 59-75.

Smith, R.E. Smoll, F.L. & Hunt, E. (1977). A system for the behavioral assessment of athletic coaches. *Research Quarterly*, **48**, pp. 401-407.

Smoll, F.L. Smith, R.E. & Hunt, E. (1978). Toward a mediational model of coach-player relationships. *Research Quarterly*, **49**, pp. 528-541.

Weiss, M.R. & Bredemeier, B.J. (1983). Developmental sport psychology: A theoretical perspective for studying children in sport. *Journal of Sport Psychology*, **5**, pp. 216-230.

Weiss, M.R. & Gould, D. (1979). *An evaluation of perceived coaching behaviors in youth sports programs in Michigan. Proceedings of the Sport Psychology Symposium* (University of Minnesota-Duluth, Duluth, Minnesota).

Non-Specialist Bibliography

Weiss, M.R. (1991). Psychological skill development in children and adolescents. *The Sport Psychologist*, **5**, 335-354.

McCullagh, P., Weiss, M.R., & Ross, D. (1989). Modeling considerations in motor skill acquisition and performance: An integrated approach. In K.B. Pandolf (Ed.) *Exercise and sport sciences reviews*, Vol. 17 (pp. 475-513). Baltimore: Williams and Wilkins.

Weiss, M.R. (1995). Children in sport: An educational model. In S. Murphy (Ed.), *Sport psychology interventions* (pp. 39-69). Champaign, IL: Human Kinetics.

Horn, T.S., & Harris, A. (1998). Perceived competence in young athletes: Research findings and recommendations for coaches and parents. In F.L. Smoll & R.E. Smith (Eds.), *Children and youth in sport: A biopsychosocial perspective* (pp. 309-329). Madison, WI: Brown & Benchmark.

Horn, T.S., Lox, C., & Labrador, F. (1998). The self-fulfilling prophecy theory: When coaches expectations become reality. In J.M. Williams (Ed.), *Applied sport psychology: Personal growth to peak performance* (3rd ed., pp. 74-91). Palo Alto, CA: Mayfield.

Passer, M.W. (1988). Determinants and consequences of children's competitive stress. In F. Smoll, R.A. Magill, & M.A. Ash (Eds.), *Children in sport* (2nd ed., pp. 203-227). Champaign, IL: Human Kinetics.

Passer, M.W. (1998). At what age are children ready to compete? Some psychological considerations. In F.L. Smoll & R.E. Smith (Eds.), *Children and youth in sport: A biopsychosocial perspective* (pp. 73-82). Madison, WI: Brown & Benchmark.

SCHOOL SPORT AND COMPETITION:
SPORTS SOCIOLOGY

School sports in America: the production of 'winners' and 'losers'

C. Roger Rees

Introduction

'All jocks stand up. We're going to kill every one of you,' the teenage killers were quoted as shouting when they entered the library during the recent massacre at Columbine High School in Littleton, Colorado (Lipsyte, 1999a). What were the motives behind this command? By killing athletes did Eric Harris and Dylan Klebold intend to strike symbolically at the heart of the school life in America, where sport typically provides the basis of school spirit and a sense of community? Or was the motive revenge against the 'put downs', bullying, and marginalization of their own group (the 'trench coat Mafia') by the jock and jock 'wannabe' groups that are usually found at the top of the social status hierarchy in the typical high school clique structure (Adler, 1999)?   Not only has the Littleton massacre fuelled nationwide debates about media violence, gun control, and secondary education in America, but it has also brought into focus tensions and paradoxes in the role played by organized sport (called interscholastic athletics) in American schools. These tensions are the subject of this paper. In it I briefly trace the origin of school sports in America, review some of the unique 'unity' rituals that have grown up around it, and show how these rituals also lead to the differentiation of the student body into cliques. I argue that in striving to use sports to symbolize students and local communities as 'winners' we also produce other groups labeled 'losers'

Correspondence to: Prof. Dr. C. Roger Rees, Department of Health Sciences, Physical Education and Human Performance Science, Adelphi University, Garden City, NY 11530, USA against which the winners are measured. I also address the argument that the elitism behind this labeling process, and the 'winning' philosophy upon which it is based, is part of the 'globalization' of sport, and is a process which is growing in other countries, not just in America. Finally, I suggest that programs in physical education that use sport as a medium for addressing moral issues and interpersonal conflicts are extremely important in contemporary education. These issues are not currently being addressed, despite the educational rhetoric used to justify sport in American schools.

We have argued elsewhere (Miracle & Rees, 1994, Chapter 1) that sport can be thought of as a powerful public ritual, a quasi-sacred experience in which people celebrate deeply held beliefs that are rarely questioned. These beliefs, which we call myths, for example that sport 'builds character' and is a positive experience for all participants, are seen as 'obvious' and 'common sense'. This mind set distracts us from investigating which experiences in sport are positive or negative, and why. In this paper I present what I consider to be a 'sociological' approach to high school sport in America, one which questions the 'common sense', 'taken-for-granted' myths behind the rituals of sport. By 'making the obvious problematic' I reveal some interesting messages about the social function of sport, which operate below the surface of more conventional interpretations. At the same time my approach is both historical, since the current status of sport can only be properly understood in a historical context, and anthropological, since it is the study of rituals in groups. By necessity the explanation of sport in schools must cross conventional disciplinary boundaries in the social sciences.

From 'play up and play the game' to 'win at all costs'

Organized sport in American schools has its origin in the athleticism movement that developed in private schools for boys in Britain (called Public Schools) in the mid- to late nineteenth century (Dunning, 1971; Mangan, 1981; Miracle & Rees, 1994, Chapter 2). During this time period a system of institutionalized games became associated with the philosophy of muscular Christianity, characterized by a belief in God, country, playing by the rules and playing fairly, and accepting amateurism as the highest form of sport. The idea that participation in sport 'built character' was the basis of this philosophy. Teachers were put in charge of sports teams and participation became compulsory. Since these activities were school sponsored they were, by definition, of educational value. As a classic example of the ritual/myth relationship, the ritual of organized school sports 'proved' the 'myth' of character building.

It is easy to see that this ritual/myth system paints a very simple picture of society, and the role of sport within it. For example, the myth that participation in sport 'builds character' is part of the 'inverted tradition' (Hobsbawm, 1983) of Britain. The rituals of sport were, and still are, used as a mirror through which we see a picture of ourselves. The British still like to think of themselves as 'fair', and as the inventors of the tradition of fair play in sport (Maguire, 1994). The real picture is much more complex and contradictory.

The muscular Christianity movement was exported to the British Empire as the graduates of the Public School system took up administrative and teaching positions in the colonies. Schools were set up for the sons of the local elites in British colonial possessions, and organized sports were practised in these schools in much the same way as in Britain (Mangan, 1986). Sport became central to the education of the sons of American elites in a similar manner, since in the mid-nineteenth century private schools following the British model were developed in the East Coast region of the United States.

The British 'play up and play the game' mentality may have been the initial philosophy behind playing sport in America, but during the late nineteenth and early twentieth century this philosophy became modified, and winning became more important (Bundgaard, 1985). Social historian Donald Mrozek (1983) has traced the origins of this 'victory philosophy' in sport to the spirit of social efficiency, the idea that individuals could work together like the parts of a machine to produce a positive social environment. Contemporary business and educational leaders in America enthusiastically accepted this philosophy. According to Mrozek (1983, p.81) victory in sport was seen as 'the greatest of all manifestations of social efficiency', and was used by political leaders of the time such as Theodore Roosevelt and Henry Cabot Lodge as a metaphor for victory by the nation in a broader political context. Sports, particularly 'American' team sports such as baseball and football, gave the opportunity for action, and as a result of action, success and victory. Winning in sport became an 'invented tradition' of America, symbolizing moral superiority and national dominance (PARK, 1987).

This winning philosophy quickly became part of organized sport at American universities, as the unique system of American intercollegiate athletics developed. During the first two decades of the twentieth century universities began to hire professional coaches whose job it was to help the sports teams win games (Mrozek, 1983; Rees, 1997). This system of intercollegiate athletics is much the same today as it was then, although now the financial stakes for the universities are much higher (Sage, 1998; Sperber, 1990).

The winning philosophy also became part of a system of high school sports organized along the same lines as college, but until recently without the high financial stakes. Sport became an essential part of the expansion of American secondary education to meet the great influx of immigrants during the early twentieth century. In America almost everyone comes from somewhere else, so the need to develop a sense of community, that is, to invent the idea of being 'American,' was an important educational goal. Sport became a valuable consensual ritual in American schools, a ritual which created a sense of solidarity and community, and it still performs this function today (Rees, 1995). There is nothing like winning sporting events to bring the school together and develop community pride. The town can collectively celebrate the success of the high school sports teams, and through that success all community members can think of themselves as 'winners'.

Rituals of unity and differentiation in American school sports

British educational sociologist Basil Bernstein was perhaps the first to apply the concept of ritual to the educative process. He identified consensual rituals responsible for developing a sense of unity and solidarity in schools, and differentiating rituals which 'mark off' or separate different groups (Bernstein, 1975, pp. 54-66). I have extended this work by showing the importance of sport in these rituals (Rees, 1995). In American schools, sport provides consensual rituals which help to unify the school around the expressive values of loyalty, hard work, obedience, and victory, but sports are also important differentiating rituals through which students get labeled 'winners' or 'losers'.

The consensual rituals of high school sport are almost unbelievable to anyone who has not experienced the American education system. I am aware of no other country in the world that celebrates unity rituals organized around school sports teams in such an intense manner. Some of these rituals, for example 'pep rallies' and 'homecoming' are unique to the American system. The pep rally reinforces the myths of victory and group cohesion. Historically the (boys) football team has been the centerpiece of this ritual, but in recent times the format may be 'modernized' to include all sports participated in by boys and girls during the semester (Fall or Spring) in which the ritual takes place. Typically, the last class on a Friday afternoon is canceled and all the students gather in the gymnasium or on the sports field. Here the athletes are honored by the teachers, administrators, students and sometimes adults from the local community. The cheerleaders perform ritual chants, and the students are encouraged by team captains, coaches and school administrators to attend the subsequent sporting events, and cheer their team on to victory (Bissinger, 1990; Burnett, 1969).

Homecoming ceremonies occur at a designated home football game. In this ritual, different groups of students might build floats that would become part of a community parade led by the school marching band before the game. Alumni are invited back to renew old ties with the school, and a Homecoming 'king' and 'queen' elected from the student body are 'crowned' during the half-time show. These students are supposed to represent high levels of morality, academic, and athletic achievement, values that are expected to be held in high esteem by the student body.

These two examples are but a sample of the rich variety of consensual rituals which usually make sport the central component of the social life of the school (for more details see Bessinger, 1990; Foley, 1990). However, because of this central importance, ability in sport is also a major source of differentiation, and figures prominently in the status hierarchy of adolescent cliques. Although these cliques are characterized by fluidity and variability as a student may be in several cliques at the same time, they are an integral part of the educational experience during adolescence (Eckert,

1989). There is also consensus about some of the basic components of clique structure. First, being a male athlete, particularly a male athlete in institutionalized team sports such as football, basketball and baseball usually ensures a student high status independent of any other characteristics. Status attached to academic, musical or other talents depends on characteristics such as personality, dress, or sports performance. The 'nerds' or brains are not usually high status (Foley, 1990).

The position of female athletes in this status hierarchy is more ambivalent. Often cheerleaders are considered high status, although this can vary from school to school, but female athletes are not assured of the high status accorded their male counterparts. Physical appearance is often an important mediating characteristic. Finally, a double standard with regard to male and female sexual behavior sometimes exists. Specifically, sexual promiscuity is often given high status in male cliques, especially among male athletes, while the same behavior among female may lead to low status labels (Foley, 1990; Rees, 1995). Sometimes the rituals of sport reinforce male superiority. For example, Foley (1990) describes the 'powder puff' football game that took place in the school he was observing at the end of the high school football season. In this game the cheerleaders and the high status senior girls put on pads and helmets, and played a 'serious' game of football. The male football players dressed up as cheerleaders, but with extra make up, short skirts and padded bras, and generally made fun of the female 'football players'. Under the guise of having fun, a role reversal ritual also became a ritual of male superiority.

It is the elitism sometimes accompanying male athletic status in schools that has drawn recent press criticism of what is called 'jock culture' in the wake of the Columbine H.S. incident. Anecdotes about male jocks bullying classmates who are physically weaker and less aggressive than themselves (Hudgins, 1999; Lipsyte, 1999a,b), and incidents in which male athletes sexually abuse female classmates (Lefkowitz, 1997; Smolowe, 1993), undermine the positive image of high school sport and the myth of character building. That scholarly research (Curry, 1998; Foley, 1990) has found such sexist values to be part of the 'culture' of sport in high schools and colleges indicates that sport plays a role in school life which is complicated and contradictory. This is not surprising given Bernstein's original thesis that schools are responsible both for developing solidarity among students, *and* separating them into different sub-groups.

School sport and the globalization of victory

Recently, global theories of sport have been concerned with the spread of the importance of achievement and victory. Some scholars have suggested that a homogenized model stressing victory is characteristic of this global spread (see reviews by Donnelly, 1996; Harvey, Rail, & Thibault, 1996; Maguire, 1994; Rees, Brettschneider, & Brandl-Bredenbeck, 1998), and this approach has also been endorsed by journalists writing for a wider audience. For example Jacques (1997) has suggested that sport has become a symbol for our changing society. Global sport, he argues, legitimates a 'winner-take-all' philosophy that has permeated all sectors of the economy from law and medicine and banking to design and fashion. Few sport sociologists would disagree with the view that 'win oriented' or 'achievement' sport is becoming a worldwide phenomenon, and that economic factors are playing a major role in its spread.

However, the empirical research, still in its infancy, shows a more complicated reality than the one suggested by economic theories alone. For example, a recent comparative study of the importance of sport and the body among German and American adolescents (Brandl-Bredenbeck, 1999; Brettschneider, Brandl-Bredenbeck, & Rees, 1996; Rees, Brettschneider, & Brandl-Bredenbeck, 1998) found evidence both for and against the salience of victory and winning as a component of sport. Specifically, Berlin and suburban New York adolescents played many of the same sports, and accepted competition and training as important characteristics of these sports. However, suburban New York adolescents had a more 'restricted' view of sport (comprising institutionalized team sports), compared to Berlin adolescents, who viewed 'leisure' activities such as skateboarding and rollerblading as legitimate sports. The Berlin adolescents also had a vaguer concept of sport than the suburban New Yorkers, one in which activities not perceived as 'win-oriented' could still be thought of as sport. We speculated that these findings were related to the fact that institutionalized team sports are so important a component of school life in America, whereas they are largely non-existent in Germany (Rees, Brettschneider, & Brandl-Bredenbeck, 1998). Our research shows some support for the idea that

American adolescents internalize a more achievement-oriented perception of sport than do German adolescents. However, it also shows that characterizations such as 'achievement' or 'win-oriented' do not do justice to the variety of associations that adolescents make with the concept of sport.

Summary: balancing 'playing to win' and 'playing for fun' in school sport

This brief review has shown that sport is a very important component of American secondary education. In many cases it is central to the social life of the school, and high school athletics often provides the most important link between the school and the wider community. Athletes are often held up as role models for younger children, as representatives of the brightest and the best that the community can produce. Interscholastic sports are accepted as being of educational value for the athletes who learn the values of winning and losing first hand, and for the rest of the students who look up to the athletes. Athletes are perceived as 'winners', since participation in athletics requires a substantial commitment of time and energy (practice is usually at least two hours a day after school during the season, and sometimes twice a day during the pre-season). Conventional wisdom has it that the positive lessons taught through athletic competition transfer to other competitive situations in life. When the high school football team wins a post-season championship (there are several classes or divisions within each State, depending on the size of the school) they are usually the center of some community-wide celebration. Set against this positive picture is a view that the emphasis on victory in school sport can subvert the educational goals of the school as athletes may be given grades so that they can remain eligible for interscholastic competition.   Furthermore, the preoccupation with winning can lead to inter-community disharmony and tension. Ethnographic studies of high school sport (e.g., Bessinger, 1990; Foley, 1990) show that these opposite forces co-exist.

The rituals of high school athletics may reinforce the 'myth' of positive character development , but this 'myth' also discourages a critical analysis of the educative role of sport in schools. If the assumption is that sport automatically teaches positive values there is little impetus to discover what, if anything, is actually being learned, or what conditions within the activity can foster values such as respect, fairness, and self-esteem (Rees,

1997).   There are no criteria for 'character development' so clearly measured as won/loss record, which is usually seen as the most important characteristic of a successful coach and team.   Programs that try to use sport to teach fairness and respect for rules (e.g., Siedentop, 1999; Gibbons, Ebbeck, & Weiss, 1995), or use the problems encountered by youth in sport to teach personal and social responsibility (Hellison, 1995, 1999), tend to be the exception rather than the rule in high school. Widespread support for such programs is diluted by the 'myth' that interscholastic athletics in its current form already produces these positive results (Rees, 1997).

In spite of this reality, or perhaps because of it, teaching social skills should be a priority in physical education (Feingold, 1994), and is being achieved by a number of innovate programs. For example, Siedentop's sport education model (1994) has been widely used and tested in different countries, and can be adapted to different curricular goals (Siedentop, 1998). Don Hellison's responsibility model uses sport as a vehicle in which students move through different levels of self-responsibility, from practicing self-control to being self-motivated and self-directed, and finally to helping others (Hellison, 1999). The recently developed curriculum guidelines for New York State (Learning Standards, 1996) are written with such social values as self-responsibility and cooperation in mind. Physical education teachers include sport and physical activity experiences in their classes that provide opportunities for student interaction through which such values can be achieved.   Similar guidelines exist at the national level (National Standards for Physical Education, 1997).   This type of curriculum development is essential to help counter the contemporary atmosphere of ultra-competitiveness in youth sport (Ferguson, 1999).

Interscholastic athletics in America has undoubtedly helped many thousands of male, and more recently female, adolescents find a sense of direction, add purpose to school life, become more motivated educationally (Fejgin, 1994), and attain access to university through athletic scholarships.   However there is nothing inevitable about the positive association between sport and success, since high school sport has also been linked to racism, sexism and elitism (Foley, 1990). In the quest for victory athletes have abused their bodies with extreme dieting (Thorton, 1990), and steroid use (Buckley et al., 1988), and educational institutions have used athletes to further their goals of victory in sport at the expense of the athletes' education (Bessinger, 1990; Frey, 1994; Joravsky, 1995). These positive and negative effects of participation in high school sport have been the subject of several REVIEWS (Miracle & Rees, 1994; Rees, in press; Rees & Miracle, in press) which have attempted to avoid the simplistic 'either/or' approach to participation (participation in sport is either 'good' or 'bad' for participants). This review has made the social function of high school athletics 'problematic', although this function is more usually seen as 'simple'. The incident at Columbine High School is a tragic reminder that we must continue to apply this 'problematic' approach to education in general. Despite the rhetoric of cooperation and cohesion behind the unity rituals, students seem not to have learned respect for individual differences, or how to avoid labeling their peers as 'winners' and 'losers'.

References
(* denotes references which may be of interest to the non-specialist)

*Adler, J. (1999, May 10). Beyond Littleton: The truth about high school. *Newsweek,* p. 56-58.

Bernstein, B. (1975). *Class, codes and control: Vol.3: Towards a theory of educational transmission.* London: Routledge & Kegan Paul.

*Bissinger, H.G. (1990). *Friday night lights: A town, a team, and a dream.* Reading, MA: Addison- Wesley.

Brandl-Bredenbeck, H.P. (1999). *Sport und jugendliches Körperkapital. Eine kulturvergleichende Untersuchung am Beispiel Deutschlands und der USA. [Sport and Adolescents' body capital - a cross-cultural comparison in Germany and the USA]* Aachen: Meyer & Meyer.

Brettschneider, W.D., Brandl-Bredenbeck, H.P., & Rees, C.R. (1996). Sportkultur von Jugendlichen in der Bundersrepublik Deutschland und in den USA - eine interkulturelle vergleichende Studie [Adolescent sports culture in the FDR and the USA - a cross cultural comparative study]. *Sportwissenschaft*, **26**, 249-271.

Buckley, W.E., Yesalis, C.E., Friedl, K.E., Anderson, W.A., Streit, A. L., & Wright, J.E. (1988). Estimated prevalence of anabolic steroid use among male high school seniors. *Journal of the American Medical Association*, **260**, 3441-3445.

Bundgaard, A. (1985): Tom Brown abroad: Athletics in selected New England Public Schools, 1850-1910. *Research Quarterly for Exercise and Sport*, Centennial Issue, **56**, 28-37.

Burnett, J. H. (1969). Ceremony, rites, and economy in the student system of an American high school. *Human Organizations*, **28**, 1-11.

Curry, T. J. (1998). Beyond the locker room: Campus bars and college athletes. *Sociology of Sport Journal*, **15**, 205-215.

Donnelly, P. (1996).   The local and the global: Globalization in the sociology of sport. *Journal of Sport and Social Issues*, **20**, 239-257.

Dunning, E. (1971). The development of modern football. In E. Dunning (Ed.) *The sociology of sport* (pp.133-51). London: Frank Cass.

*Eckert, P. (1989). *Jocks and burnouts: Social categories and identity in the high school.* New York: Teachers College Press.

Feingold, R.S. (1994).   Making connections: An agenda for the future. *Quest*, **46**, 356-367.

Fejgin, N. (1994).   Participation in high school competitive sports: A subversion of school mission or contribution to academic goals? *Sociology of Sport Journal*, **11**, 211-230.

*Ferguson, A. (1999, July 12).   Inside the crazy culture of kids sports. *Time*, pp. 52-62.

Foley, D. (1990). The great American football ritual: Reproducing race, class and gender inequality. *Sociology of Sport Journal*, **7**, 111-135.

*Frey. D. (1994). *The last shot: City streets, basketball dreams.* Boston: Houghton Mifflin.

Gibbons, S., Ebbeck, V., & Weiss, M. (1995). Fair play for kids: Effects on the moral development of children in physical education.   *Research Quarterly for Exercise and Sport*, **66**, 247-255.

Harvey, J., Rail, G., & Thibault, L.   (1996).   Globalization and sport. Sketching a theoretical model for empirical research. *Journal of Sport and Social Issues*, **20**, 258-277.

Hellison, D. (1999). Teaching responsibility in school physical education. In R. Feingold, C. R. Rees, G. Barrette, L. Fiorentino, S. Virgilio, & E. Kowalski (Eds.), *Education for life. AIESEP/Adelphi Proceedings* (pp. 276-280). Garden City, New York, Adelphi University.

Hellison, D. (1995). *Teaching responsibility through physical activity.* Champaign, IL: Human Kinetics.

Hobsbawm, E. (1983). Introduction – inventing traditions. In E. Hobsbawm and T. Ranger (Eds.), *The invention of tradition* (pp. 1-14). Cambridge: Cambridge University Press.

*Hudgins, A. (1999, May 1). When bullies ruled the hallways. *The New York Times*, p. A15.

*Jacques, M. (1997, July 13). Worshipping the body at the altar of sport. *The London Observer*, pp. 18-19.

*Joravsky, D. (1995). *Hoop dreams: A true story of leadership and triumph.* Atlanta, GA: Turner Publishing Company.

Learning standards for physical education. The New York State Education Department, 1996.

*Lefkowitz, B. (1997). *Our guys: The Glen Ridge rape and the secret life of the perfect suburb.* Berkeley, CA.: University of California Press.

*Lipsyte, R. (1999a, May 9). The jock culture: Time to debate the questions. *The New York Times*, Section 8, p. 11.

*Lipsyte, R. (1999b, May 23). The entangled web around youth sports. *The New York Times*, Section 8, p. 13.

Maguire, J. (1994). Sport, identity politics and globalization: Diminishing contrasts and increasing varieties. *Sociology of Sport Journal*, **11**, 398-427.

Mangan, J.A. (1981). *Athleticism in the Victorian and Edwardian public school.* Cambridge: Cambridge University Press.

Mangan, J.A. (Ed.) (1986). *The games ethic and imperialism.* New York: Viking Press.

*Miracle, A. W., & Rees, C. R. (1994). *Lessons of the locker room: The myth of school sports*. Amherst, NY: Prometheus.

Mrozek, D.J. (1983). *Sport and American mentality*, 1880-1910. Knoxville: The University of Tennessee Press.

National standards for physical education. National Association for Physical Education and Sport , AAHPERD, 1997.

Park, R. (1987). Sport, gender and society in a transatlantic Victorian perspective. In J.A. Mangan & R. Park (Eds.), *From 'fair sex' to feminism: Sport and the socialization of women in the industrial and post-industrial eras* (pp. 58-93). London: Frank Cass.

Rees, C. R. (in press). 'Sport and schooling.' In David L. Levinson, Alan R. Sadovnik and Peter W. Cookson, Jr. (Eds.) *Education and Sociology: An Encyclopedia.* New York: Garland.

Rees, C.R. (1997). Still building American character: Sport and the physical education curriculum. *The Curriculum Journal*, **8**, 199-212.

Rees, C.R. (1995). What price victory? Myths, rituals, athletics and the dilemma of schooling. In A. Sadovnik (Ed.) *Knowledge and pedagogy: The sociology of Basil Bernstein* (pp.371-378). Norwood, NJ.: Ablex.

Rees, C.R., Brettschneider, W.D., & Brandl-Bredenbeck, H.P. (1998). Globalization of sports activities and perceptions of sport among adolescents from Berlin and suburban New York. *Sociology of Sport Journal*, **15,** 216-230.

Rees, C. R., & Miracle A. W. (in press). Sport and education. In J. Coakley & E. Dunning (Eds.), *Handbook of sport and society*. London: Sage.

Sage, G. H. (1998). *Power and Ideology in American Sport*, 2nd Edition, Champaign, IL.: Human Kinetics.

Siedentop D. (1999). Sport education: A retrospective. In R. Feingold, C. R. Rees, G. Barrette, L. Fiorentino, S. Virgilio, & E. Kowalski (Eds.), *Education for life. AIESEP/Adelphi Proceedings* (pp. 102-108). Garden City, New York, Adelphi University.

Siedentop, D. (1994). *Sport education: Quality PE through positive experiences*. Champaign, IL: Human Kinetics.

Smolowe, J. (1993, April 5). Sex without a score card. *Time*, p. 41.

Sperber, M. (1990). *College sports inc.: The athletic department vs. the university*. New York: Henry Holt.

Thornton, (1990). Feast or famine: Eating disorders in athletics. *Physician and Sports Medicine*, **18**, 116-122.

INFORMATION SECTION

Resources and Contacts in Physical Education

1. INTERNATIONAL ORGANISATIONS

ICSSPE - International Council of Sport Science and Physical Education

ICSSPE is an umbrella organisation unique in its membership structure. A diverse range of 200 member organisations from 60 nations world-wide, spanning governmental bodies, international sport/sport science organisations, non-governmental organisations (NGO's) and universities/ research centres are linked within the Council. An Associations' Board, consisting of 14 international organisations to date, directs ICSSPE's work.

ICSSPE is the only NGO in the area of sport science and physical education working in formal associate relations with UNESCO. The Council also works closely with the IOC and WHO. In addition to facilitating communication and the exchange of information world-wide in all areas of sport science and physical education, ICSSPE produces scientific and practical publications, and organises the Pre-Olympic Scientific Congress every four years just prior to the Olympic Summer Games.

Physical Education is a priority area within ICSSPE and the Council is addressing the current crisis in Physical Education on a world scale by organising the World Summit on Physical Education from November 3-5, 1999, in Berlin.

ICSSPE/CIEPSS Executive Office	Tel: +49 30 805 00360
Am Kleinen Wannsee 6	Fax: +49 30 805 6386
14109 Berlin	E-mail: icsspe@icsspe.org
GERMANY	Internet: www.icsspe.org

ICSP - International Committee of Sport Pedagogy

ICSP was established as an ICSSPE committee in 1984, connecting the following 5 international organisations: - AIESEP, FIEP, IAPESGW, IFAPA, ISCPES – (descriptions and contact information below). Leadership of the Committee rotates through the 5 organisations. Currently, Mr. John Andrews, the President of FIEP is the ICSP Chairperson and the Secretariat is managed by IAPESGW:

ICSP Secretariat	
Prof. Dr. Margaret Talbot, IAPESGW President	
Leeds Metropolitan University	
Beckett Park Campus	Tel: +44 113 283 7431
LS6 3QS Leeds	Fax: +44 113 283 7430
UNITED KINGDOM	E-mail: M.Talbot@LMU.ac.uk

ICSP regularly produces publications and has recently undertaken a research project addressing the silent crisis of physical education. The study, 'The State and Status of Physical Education in a Global Context' is being funded by the IOC and its results will be presented at the Berlin World Summit on Physical Education in November 1999. For more information about this research project, contact:

Dr. Ken Hardman	Tel: +44 1612 754962
Centre for PE and Leisure Studies	Fax: +44 1612 753519
University of Manchester, Oxford Rd.	E-mail: Kenneth.hardman@man.ac.uk
M139PL Manchester, UK	Internet: www.man.ac.uk/education/pecrisis

1.1 ICSP MEMBER ORGANISATIONS:

AIESEP - Association Internationale des Ecoles Supérieures d'Education Physique

AIESEP is a non-governmental professional organisation of universities and institutions supporting physical education, sport science and sport pedagogy. AIESEP's purpose is to promote the integration of knowledge in sport sciences. Through its publications and regular conferences it recognises the close relationship among scholarship, research, professional preparation, and professional practice.

Dr. Ron Feingold, AIESEP President	
Adelphi University, Dept. of Health Studies,	Tel: +1 516 877 4262
P.E. & Human Performance Science	Fax: +1 516 877 4258
Garden City, New York , 11530 USA	E-mail: Feingold@adlibv.adelphi.edu

FIEP - Fédération Internationale de l'Education Physique

Founded in 1923 in Brussels, the aim of the Federation is to promote the development of a broad range of activities in the fields of Education, Physical Education, and Sports Education, Sports for All, Fitness and Health, Recreation and the use and protection of the Outdoors, and to contribute to international co-operation in these fields. FIEP provides a network of contacts and a means of communication and exchange amongst individuals and organisations in 120 countries. It has 'Recognised Organisation' status with the International Olympic Committee and maintains close working relationships with UNESCO, WHO, and the Arab Confederation of Sport (ASC), l'Union Arabe de l'Education Physique et du Sport (UAEPS) and, more recently, with the Foundation for Olympic and Sport Education (FOSE) and the International Institute of the Rights of the Child (IDE). The annual programme of events, meetings, projects and other activities organised or supported by the Federation concern the scientific, technical, teaching and management aspects of physical education, sport, physical recreation, fitness and health.

The principle means of action in FIEP are:
- Publication of the trimestrial, trilingual (English/French/Spanish) *FIEP Bulletin*, now in its 69th year of publication;
- Regional and Ad hoc Commissions;
- Practical courses, congresses, and symposia;
- Exchange travel facilitated for both individuals and groups;
- Research, Documentation and Information Exchange with other national and international bodies; and
- The HRH Prince Faisal Prize (in association with the ASC) - prizes totalling US$30,000 US.

Mr. John Andrews, FIEP President	
Les Loges	Tel: +33 549 439359
86470 Montreuil Bonnin	Fax: +33 549 439359
France	E-mail: Jcafiepics@aol.com

IFAPA - International Federation of Adapted Physical Activity

IFAPA was founded in Québec, Canada in 1973. Since then it has rapidly expanded to become a cross-disciplinary professional organisation of individuals, institutions, and agencies world-wide supporting and promoting adapted physical activity (APA), disability sport and all aspects of sport, movement and exercise science for individuals with diverse needs. Its members are specialists, researchers, professors, scientists and students of disciplines as varied as: physical education, recreation and leisure, sport training, physical therapy, medicine, biomechanics, nutrition, occupational therapy, and gerontology.

The purposes of IFAPA are to encourage international co-operation in the field of physical activity to the benefit of individuals of all abilities; to promote, stimulate and support research in the field of adapted physical activity throughout the world; and to make scientific knowledge of and practical experiences in APA available to all interested persons, organisations and institutions. IFAPA co-ordinates national, regional, and international functions (both governmental and non-governmental) that pertain to sport, dance, aquatics, exercise, fitness and wellness for individuals of all ages with disabilities and special needs. It also organises international symposia every two years.

The Adapted Physical Activity Quarterly (APAQ) is the official journal of IFAPA. Other publications include Symposia proceedings and a quarterly newsletter.

Prof. Dr. Karen DePauw, IFAPA Past-President	
Graduate School	Tel: +1 509 3356424
Washington State University	Fax: +1 509 3351949
99 164-1030 Pullman, WA, USA	E-mail: kpdepauw@wsu.edu

IAPESGW - International Association of Physical Education and Sport for Girls and Women

Founded in 1948, IAPESGW brings together women from countries world-wide who are working in sport and physical education. The founders and its first President, Dorothy Ainsworth, believed in the need for an international network to promote physical education for women throughout the world. IAPESGW now represents the interests of girls and women at all levels of sport and physical education through its network of members, publications and conferences. Every two years the Association organises conferences to offer women a forum to present research, advance practice, network and share experiences.

Prof. Dr. Margaret Talbot, IAPESGW President	
Leeds Metropolitan University	Tel: +44 113 283 7431
Beckett Park Campus	Fax: +44 113 283 7430
LS6 3QS Leeds, UK	E-mail: M.Talbot@LMU.ac.uk

ISCPES - International Society of Comparative Physical Education and Sport

ISCPES was founded in 1978 in Israel. Since then it has made significant progress - in addition to its Biennial Conferences and the regular publication of the *Journal of Comparative Physical Education and Sport*, the Society's members have been, and continue to be, active in comparative research studies involving teams of individuals and network groups. The Society has produced a number of monographs, and publishes proceedings from all of its Conferences. The first volume of a new book series, focusing on specific countries will be published in the Spring of 1999: 'Physical Education and Sport in China' (J. Riordan and R. Jones, Eds). Subsequent volumes will cover Germany, Australia, S. Africa, and themes/topics such as Women and Sport, Adapted Physical Activity and Comparative P.E. and Sport Methodology.

Dr. Ken Hardman, ISCPES Past President	Tel: +44 1612 754962
Centre for PE and Leisure Studies	Fax: +44 1612 753519
University of Manchester, Oxford Road	E-mail: Kenneth.hardman@man.ac.uk
M139PL Manchester, UK	Internet: http://ISCPES.uwo.ca

1.2 OTHER INTERNATIONAL ORGANISATIONS

ICHPER.SD - International Council for Health, Physical Education, Recreation, Sport and Dance

ICHPER-SD represents professionals in health, physical education, recreation, sport and dance. It consists of seven regional organisations (Africa, Asia, Europe, Latin America, Middle East, North America and

Caribbean, and Oceania), and 32 commissions of specialisations/ disciplines. ICHPER-SD publishes a quarterly journal and organises world conferences uniting members in 145 countries.

Dr. Dong Ja Yang, ICHPER-SD Secretary General	
Averett College	
301 North Washington Street	Tel: +1 703 237 1560
Falls Church, Virginia 22046, USA	Fax: +1 703 538 6373

ACAPS - Association des Chercheurs en Activités Physiques et Sportives

L'ACAPS est une association francophone regroupant des chercheurs, essentiellement des universitaires, travaillant sur les activités physiques et sportives. Ses membres se recrutent dans toutes les disciplines, de la physiologie à l'histoire, en passant par la biomécanique, la médecine, les neurosciences, la psychologie , les sciences de l'éducation et la sociologie.

Prof. Dr. Michel Laurent, Président	Tel: +33 0491 17 22 50
Faculté des Sciences du Sport	Fax: +33 0491 17 22 52
163, avenue de Luminy	E-mail: Laurent@laps.univ-mrs.fr
13009 Marseille Cedex, FRANCE	Internet: www.bham.ac.uk/sportex/ACAPS/

1.3 REGIONAL ORGANISATIONS

AAHPERD - American Association of Health, Physical Education, Recreation and Dance

Dr. Michael G. Davis	Tel: +1 703 476 3404
Executive Vice President	Fax: +1 703 476 9527
1900 Association Drive	E-mail: mgdavis@aahperd.org
Reston, Virginia 20191-1598, USA	Internet: www.aahperd.org

AFAHPER-SD - African Association of Health, Physical Education, Recreation and Dance

Prof. Moni Wekesa	
Secretary General	
P.O. Box 56192	Tel and Fax: +254 2 883525
Nairobi, KENYA	E-mail: wekesa@insightkenya.com

ENSSHE - European Network of Sport Science in Higher Education
REISS - Réseau Européen des Instituts de Sciences du Sport

ENSSHE Secretariat	
Ms. Elena Gil	Tel: +34 93 4255445
C/o INEFC, Av. De l'Estadi, s/n	Fax: +34 93 426 1589
08038 Barcelona, SPAIN	E-mail: euronet@correu.gencat.es

Dr. Willy Laporte	
Coordinator, PE Committee, ENSSHE	
Universiteit Gent	
Watersportlaan 2	Tel: +32 9 264 63 31
9000 Gent, BELGIUM	Fax: +32 9 264 64 84

ECSS - European College of Sport Science

Prof. Dr. Joachim Mester, President	
Deutsche Sporthochschule Köln	Tel: +49 221 4982209
Carl-Diem-Weg 6	Fax: +49 221 4971130
50933 Köln, GERMANY	E-mail: mester@hrz.dshs-koeln.de

EUPEA - European Union of Physical Education Associations

Dr. Richard Fisher, President	
St. Mary's University College	
Department of Sport, Health and Exercise Science	Tel: +44 181 240 4183
Strawberry Hill, Twickenham	Fax: +44 181 240 4212
TW1 4SX Middx. UK	E-mail: fisherr@smuc.ac.uk

2. PUBLICATIONS

2.1 Journals

- ◆ African Journal for Physical, Health Education, Recreation and Dance
- ◆ Australian Journal of Health, Physical Education and Recreation
- ◆ Asian Journal of Physical Education
- ◆ British Journal of Physical Education
- ◆ Education Physique et Sport

- European Journal of Physical Education
- European Physical Education Review
- International Journal of Physical Education
- Japanese Journal of Physical Education
- Journal of Comparative Physical Education and Sport
- Journal of Physical Education, Recreation and Dance
- Journal of Teaching in Physical Education
- Quest
- South African Journal of Physical Education
- Sportunterricht

2.2 Book Series

Important and high quality book series have been published by some national P.E. or sport science associations like the American Association of Health, Physical Education and Dance (AAHPERD) in the U.S.A, the Physical Education Association of the United Kingdom (PEAUK), the AFRAPS (France), and the Deutsche Vereinigung f. Sportwissenschaft (DVS) in Germany, as well as by some international publishing houses in the field of Physical Education and Sport Pedagogy e.g. Human Kinetics, Meyer & Meyer Sport, Hofmann, Spon. Numerous series within and outside these publishing houses are produced to introduce, promote, develop and enhance specific physical activities and sports at different performance levels.

3. INTERNET RESOURCES

3.1 Multilingual

SportQuest
<http://www.SPORTQuest.com>
SPORTQuest is an important 'first stop' for sport, sport science and physical education information on the Web. This site contains high quality links in many languages. It is produced and updated by the Sport Information Resource Centre (SIRC) in Canada. Physical Education is included in the List of Topics under Sport Science.

SIRC/ICSSPE Conference Calendar
<www.SPORTQuest.com/sirc/calen.html>
A current list of forthcoming international congresses, conferences, symposia, and seminars dealing with sport science and physical education. Updated weekly.

3.2 English

Legal Issues in Physical Education
<http://www.cortland.edu/www/libwww/legal_issues_pe.html>
Updated regularly, this site includes periodical articles, books in general, case books, law books and court decisions and other Internet links.

PE Central
<http//pe.central.vt.edu>
Includes a wide range of information, including: lesson plans and assessment ideas; professional information; books and software; instructional resources; children's quotes and additional WWW links.

Physical Education Digest
<http://domains.cyberbeach.net/pedigest/>
A 36-page quarterly magazine that provides the latest ideas, tips, coaching cues and research on sports, fitness and physical education topics from around the world - condensed into brief, easy-to-understand articles. Each issue represents the best information selected from almost 5000 pages of original material. It's quick, easy to read and very practical.

Sports Media
<http://www.ping.be/sportsmedia/>
A tool for PE teachers, coaches, students and everybody who is interested in sport. Provides links to PE lesson plans, coaching & training sites and other sports topics.

Coaching Youth Sports
<http://www.chre.vt.edu/f-s/rstratto/CYS/>
An electronic newsletter for coaches, athletes and parents. The purpose is to present information about learning and performing sport skills. This information comes mostly from the motor skill learning and sport

psychology areas of the sport sciences. The primary focus is on the 6-16 age range, but topics related to high school athletes may also be discussed. Links to other useful Internet sites are also included.

Educator Resources – Physical Education
<http://www.mcrel.org/resources/links/pe.asp>
A comprehensive and easy to use general reference library of online dictionaries, encyclopaedias, thesauri, atlases, electronic texts and more.

Listserves in Physical Education
<http://educ.ubc.ca/faculty/lstanley/pe/listserves.html>

3.3 Spanish

ÁSKESIS
<http://www.askesis.arrakis.es
El lugar de encuentro de todas las personas allegadas al mundillo de la Educación Física y los Deportes" / Spanish physical education journal.

Spain: La Educación Física en España
<http://www.adi.uam.es/~vmartha/ef1.html>

3.4 French

Education Physique et Sportive (EPS)
<http://www.ac-nancy-metz.fr/enseign/EPS/EPS.htm>
Site permettant aux enseignant d'EPS de se procurer des ressources pédagogiques et didactiques.

Les listes de diffusion francophones
<http://www.cru.fr/listes>

3.5 German

Physical Education - Sportpedagogic Online
<http://members.aol.com/rolfdober/sportpaed/index.html>
Das Internet als sportpädagogisches Nachschlagwerk und Diskussionsforum Sportunterricht - Sportpädagogik im Internet.

ICSSPE

CIEPSS

International Council of Sport Science and Physical Education (ICSSPE)

Join ICSSPE!

If your organisation wishes to:
➤ Benefit from the experience of others
➤ Contribute its own experience for the benefit of others
➤ Become part of the international network of physical education and sport science,

Join the International Council of Sport Science and Physical Education!
ICSSPE admits members in four categories:
A) Governmental organisations and non-governmental bodies that are the major organisations responsible for sport or sport science in their respective countries.
B) International organisations working to unify, co-ordinate, and promote activities in the field of physical education and sport: (a) international organisations concerned with sport science, physical education, sport and recreation; (b) international sport federations; (c) international organisations (cultural, artistic, scientific) with an interest in sport and physical education.
C) National non-governmental organisations concerned with sport science, physical education, sport and recreation.
D) Research institutes and schools of higher learning in physical education or sport science.

Currently more than 200 organisations and institutions form all parts of the world are affiliated with ICSSPE.

Please return the completed membership application to:

ICSSPE/CIEPSS
Am Kleinen Wannsee 6
14109 Berlin
GERMANY

Tel: +49 30 805 00360
Fax: +49 30 805 6386
E-mail: icsspe@icsspe.or
Internet: www.icsspe.org

ICSSPE Membership Application

I hereby apply for the membership of the:

_____

_____

(name of organisation/institution)

Full address of organisation/institution:

_____

_____

_____

_____

_____

Telephone:_____ Fax:_____

E-mail:_____ Internet:_____

Name and function of responsible representative:

_____

_____

My organisation /institution is: Annual
                                                    Membership Fee

❑   A. The major governmental/non-governmental body   US$350
        responsible for sport or sport science in my country.

❑   B. International organisation of sport, sport science,   US$200
        or physical education.

❑   C. A national governmental/non-governmental organ-   US$150
        isation of sport, sport science or physical education.

❑   D. A research institute or school of higher learning   US$80
        in sport, sport science or physical education.

Membership fee includes a free subscription to all ICSSPE publications. For a complete listing please visit our Website.

Payment: ❑ by cheque   ❑ by money transfer

Signature:_____ Date:_____

ulletin

ICSSPE Bulletin

A magazine produced by the ICSSPE addressing all areas of sport science and physical education and presenting research, congress reports, newly published resources and initiatives that ICSSPE and its members are involved in.

Two issues/year, 68 pages
Single copy: US$ 10.- plus shipping

Annual subsciption rate:
1999: US$ 19.- plus shipping (2 Volumes)
2000: US$ 28,- plus shipping (3 Volumes)

MEYER & MEYER SPORT

Von-Coels-Str. 390 · 52080 Aachen · Germany · Hotline: ++49-180-5 10 11 15
http://www.meyer-meyer-sports.com

Please accept my subscription order for **"ICSSPE Bulletin"** (calender year only)

Name: _____

Address: _____

_____

_____

__ Visa __ Eurocard/Mastercard __ American Express

Number _____ Expiry Date ___ . ___

Date, Signature: _____

Make payments by credit card, international money order or postal order and send to the address above, send a fax to ++49/241/ 9 58 10 10 or e-mail to verlag@meyer-meyer-sports.com